Russian cases

Made simple

Artemiy Belyaev

Edition 1, December 2017

Table of contents

Introduction

Grammatical cases are usually the most difficult part of Russian language learning, and this book was written to help you to master them.

In order to use this book, you should know the basic grammar of the Russian language, because this book is only about cases.

What this book consists of:

Chapters about case declension of pronouns, nouns, adjectives, numerals, question words – these chapters are about which word form one must use with the appropriate case; Chapters about each of the 6 main cases with all ways of use; Chapters about additional cases about which you probably have not heard; Exercises.

Vowels in stressed syllables of Russian words are marked by bold font weight;

Sections of examples have translations of many words after each sentence.

Abbreviations of grammatical genders and plural:

(m) – masculine, (f)- feminine, (n)- neuter, (pl) - plural

How to use this book

There is not a fixed order of learning in this book. You can begin from any part of this book and jump to any chapter whenever you want.

When you read examples of case use or do exercises, you can always check proper declensions in the chapters about declension of pronouns, nouns, adjectives, etc.

I recommend declining 30-50 nouns and adjectives by cases in order to know which ending to use with each case automatically before learning case use.

What is a Grammatical Case?

Grammatical cases express grammatical functions of nouns, adjectives, pronouns, participles, and numerals. That's why the word order in Russian sentences is not as important as it is in English and other language that don't have cases.

Cases describe relationships between a verb and an object, between two nouns, between a preposition and a noun, and other parts of speech.

In order to understand the concept of cases simpler, let's consider cases in the English language. There are cases in English, however only some pronouns have them:

I - me;

He – him;

She – her;

We – us;

They – them;

The pronouns "me, him, her, us, them" are the pronouns "I, he, she, we, they" declined by cases. But in the Russian language, not only pronouns are declined, but also nouns, adjectives, pronouns, participles, and numerals.

Declension of question words

Nom.	Кто - who	Что - what	Чей - whose
Gen.	Кого	Чего	Чьего
Dat.	Кому	Чему	Чьему
Acc.	Кого	Что	Чей/Чьего
Inst.	Кем	Чем	Чьим
Prep.	О ком	О чём	О чьём

Какой(m) , Какая(f), Какое(n), Какие(pl) – What/which

Nom.	Какой	Какая	Какое	Какие
Gen.	Какого	Какой	Какого	Каким
Dat.	Какому	Какой	Какому	Каких
Acc.	Какой / Какого	Какую	Какое	Каких / Какие
Inst.	Каким	Какой	Каким	Какими
Prep.	О каком	О какой	О каком	О каких

Который(m), Которая(f), Которое(n), Которые(pl) - Which

Nom.	Который	Которая
Gen.	Которого	Которой
Dat.	Которому	Которой
Acc.	Который / Которого	Которую
Inst.	Которым	Которой
Prep.	О котором	О которой

Nom.	**Которое**	**Которые**
Gen.	Которого	Которых
Dat.	Которому	Которым
Acc.	Которое	Которых / Которые
Inst.	Которым	Которыми
Prep.	О котором	О которых

Declension of pronouns

Personal pronouns

Nom.	Я - I	Ты - You	Он - He	Она - She
Gen.	Меня	Тебя	Его/него	Её
Dat.	Мне	Тебе	Ему/нему	Ей/ней
Acc.	Меня	Тебя	Его/него	Её/неё
Inst.	Мной	Тобой	Им/ним	Ей/ней
Prep.	О мне	О тебе	О нём	О ней

Nom.	Мы - We	Вы – You	Они - They
Gen.	Нас	Вас	Их
Dat.	Нам	Вам	Им
Acc.	Нас	Вас	Их
Inst.	Нами	Вами	Ими
Prep.	О нас	О вас	О них

Reflexive personal pronouns

The reflexive pronoun Себя is the same for all personal pronouns and has the same form in all cases:

Nom.	Себя
Gen.	Себя
Dat.	Себя
Acc.	Себя
Inst.	Себя
Prep.	Себя

But these reflexive pronouns are declined by cases:

Сам (m), Сама (f), Само (n), Сами (pl)

Nom.	Сам (m)	Сама (f)	Само (n)	Сами (pl)
Gen.	Самого	Самой	Самого	Самих
Dat.	Самому	самой	Самому	Самим
Acc.	Самого	Саму	Самого	Самих
Inst.	Самим	Самой	Самим	Самими
Prep.	О самом	О самой	О самом	О самих

Possessive pronouns

Мой(m), моя(f), моё(n), мои(pl) – my/mine

Nom.	Мой - My	Моя	Моё	Мои
Gen.	Моего	Моей	Моего	Моих
Dat.	Моему	Моей	Моему	Моим
Acc.	Мой / моего	Мою	Моё	Мои / моих
Inst.	Моим	Моей	Моим	Моими
Prep.	О моём	О моей	О моём	О моих

Твой(m), твоя(f), твоё(n), твои(pl) – your/yours

Nom.	Твой - your	Твоя	Твоё	Твои
Gen.	Твоего	Твоей	Твоего	Твоих
Dat.	Твоему	Твоей	Твоему	Твоим
Acc.	Твой/ твоего	Твою	Твоё	Твои/ твоих
Inst.	Твоим	Твоей	Твоим	Твоими
Prep.	О твоём	О твоей	О твоём	О твоих

Наш(m), наша(f), наше(n), наши(pl) – our/ours

Nom.	Наш - our	Наша	Наше	Наши
Gen.	Нашего	Нашей	Нашего	Наших
Dat.	Нашему	Нашей	Нашему	Нашим
Acc.	Наш/ нашего	Нашу	Наш	Наши/ наших
Inst.	Нашим	Нашей	Нашим	Нашими
Prep.	О нашем	О нашей	О нашем	О наших

Ваш(m), ваша(f), ваше(n), ваши(pl) – your/yours

Nom.	Ваш	Ваша	Ваше	Ваши
Gen.	Вашего	Вашей	Вашего	Ваших
Dat.	Вашему	Вашей	Вашему	Вашим
Acc.	Ваш/ вашего	Вашу	Ваш	Ваши/ ваших
Inst.	Вашим	Вашей	Вашим	Вашими
Prep.	О вашем	О вашей	О вашем	О ваших

Reflexive possessive pronouns

Свой(m), Своя(f), Своё(n), Свои(pl)

Nom.	Свой	Своя	Своё	Свои
Gen.	Своего	Своей	Своего	Своих
Dat.	Своему	Свою	Своему	Своим
Acc.	Своего / Свой	Свою	Своё	Своих / Свои
Inst.	Своим	Своей	Своём	Своими
Prep.	О своём	О своей	О своём	О своих

Demonstrative pronouns

Nom.	Этот(m) - this	Эта(f) – this	Это(n) - this	Эти(pl) - these
Gen.	Этого	Этой	Этого	Этих
Dat.	Этому	Этой	Этому	Этим
Acc.	Этот / Этого	Эту	Это	Эти / Этих
Inst.	Этим	Этой	Этим	Этими
Prep.	Об этом	Об этой	Об этом	Об этих

Nom.	Тот(m) - that	Та(f) - that	То(n) - that	Те(pl) - those
Gen.	Того	Той	Того	Тех
Dat.	Тому	Той	Тому	Тем
Acc.	Того / тот	Ту	То	Тех / те
Inst.	Тем	Той	Тем	Теми
Prep.	О том	О той	О том	О тех

Declension of numerals

The numeral *ОДИН* – *one* has masculine, feminine, neuter forms. And it is applied in pair with decimals (21, 31, 41, 51… and so on up to infinity)

The numeral ДВА – *two* has only plural and feminine forms. These forms are applied in pair with decimals (22, 32, 42, 52…. And so on up to infinity).

All next numerals have only single genderless form.

Declension of the numeral ОДИН – one (1):

Nom.	Один(m) - one	Одна(f) - one	Одно(n) - one
Gen.	Одного	Одной	Одного
Dat.	Одному	Одной	Одному
Acc.	Одного / один	Одну	Одно
Inst.	Одним	Одной	Одним
Prep.	Об одном	Об одной	Об одном

Declension of the numeral ДВА – two (2):

It differs only in nominative and accusative cases, all other cases match

Nom.	Два (m/n/pl) - two	Две (f) - two
Gen.	Двух	Двух
Dat.	Двум	Двум
Acc.	Двух / два	Две
Inst.	Двумя	Двумя
Prep.	О двух	О двух

Declension of all next numerals:

Nom.	**Три - 3**	**Четыре - 4**	**Пять - 5**
Gen.	Трёх	Четырёх	Пяти
Dat.	Трём	Четырём	Пяти
Acc.	Трёх / три	Четырёх / четыре	Пять
Inst.	Тремя	Четырьмя	Пятью
Prep.	О трёх	О четырёх	О пяти

Nom.	**Шесть - 6**	**Семь - 7**	**Восемь - 8**	**Девять - 9**
Gen.	Шести	Семи	Восьми	Девяти
Dat.	Шести	Семи	Восьми	Девяти
Acc.	Шесть	Семь	Восемь	Девять
Inst.	Шестью	Семью	Восемью	Девятью
Prep.	О шести	О семи	О восьми	О девяти

Nom.	**Десять - 10**	**Одиннадцать -11**
Gen.	Десяти	Одиннадцати
Dat.	Десяти	Одиннадцати
Acc.	Десять	Одиннадцать
Inst.	Десятью	Одиннадцатью
Prep.	О десяти	Об одиннадцати

Next numerals from 12 to 30 will have the same case endings as ОДИННАДЦАТЬ – 11:

Двенадцать – 12

Тринадцать -13

Четырнадцать -14

Пятнадцать – 15

Шестнадцать – 16

Семнадцать – 17

Восемнадцать – 18

Девятнадцать – 19

Двадцать -20

Тридцать – 30

Let's consider the next ones – СОРОК – 40, ПЯТЬДЕСЯТ – 50.
СОРОК – 40 is an exception that requires memorization, it doesn't have –*десят* in it.

Nom.	**СОРОК - 40**
Gen.	Сорока
Dat.	Сорока
Acc.	Сорок
Inst.	Сорока
Prep.	О сорока

And let's consider ПЯТЬДЕС**Я**Т - 50, ШЕСТЬДЕС**Я**Т - 60, СЕМЬДЕС**Я**Т - 70, В**О**СЕМЬДЕС**Я**Т - 80, ДЕВЯН**О**СТО – 90:

The unique one is only ДЕВЯН**О**СТО - 90 here, because it doesn't have the same ending as 50, 60, 70, 80.

Formula for memorizing 50, 60, 70, 80:

ПЯТЬДЕС**Я**Т consists of ПЯТЬ(5) and ДЕСЯТЬ(10)

ШЕСТЬДЕС**Я**Т consists of ШЕСТЬ(6) and ДЕСЯТЬ(10)

СЕМЬДЕС**Я**Т consists of СЕМЬ(7) and ДЕСЯТЬ(10)

В**О**СЕМЬДЕС**Я**Т consists of В**О**СЕМЬ(8) and ДЕСЯТЬ(10)

It means that 50, 60, 70, 80 will be declined as a sum of numbers it consists of:

Nom.	**ПЯТЬДЕС**Я**Т - 50**	**ШЕСТЬДЕС**Я**Т - 60**
Gen.	Пят**и**десят**и**	Шестидесяти
Dat.	Пят**и**десят**и**	Шестидесяти
Acc.	Пятьдес**я**т	шестьдесят
Inst.	Пять**ю**десят**ью**	Шестьюдесятью
Prep.	О пят**и**десят**и**	О шестидесяти

Nom.	**СЕМЬДЕС**Я**Т - 70**	**В**О**СЕМЬДЕС**Я**Т - 80**
Gen.	Семидесяти	Восьмидесяти
Dat.	Семидесяти	Восьмидесяти
Acc.	Семьдесят	Восемьдесят
Inst.	Семьюдесятью	Восьмьюдесятью
Prep.	О семидесяти	О восьмидесяти

You can see, that the numerals 50, 60, 70, 80 are declined as 5, 6, 7, 8 placed together with 10.

And finally, let's decline 90 and 100 and 200

Nom.	Девяносто - 90	Сто - 100
Gen.	Девяноста	Ста
Dat.	Девяноста	Ста
Acc.	Девяносто	Сто
Inst.	Девяносто	Ста
Prep.	О девяноста	О ста

Nom.	Двести - 200	Триста - 300	Четыреста - 400
Gen.	Двухсот	Трёхсот	Четырёхсот
Dat.	Двумстам	Трёмстам	Четырёмстам
Acc.	Двести	Триста	Четыреста
Inst.	Двумястами	Тремястами	Четырьмястами
Prep.	О двухстах	О трёхстах	О четырёхстах

Nom.	Пятьсот - 500	Шестьсот - 600	Семьсот - 700
Gen.	Пятисот	Шестисот	Семисот
Dat.	Пятистам	Шестистам	Семистам
Acc.	Пятьсот	Шестьсот	Семьсот
Inst.	Пятьюстами	Шестьюстами	Семьюстами
Prep.	О пятистах	О шестистах	О семистах

Nom.	**Восемьсот - 800**	**Девятьсот - 900**
Gen.	Восьмисот	Девятисот
Dat.	Восьмистам	Девятистам
Acc.	Восемьсот	Девятьсот
Inst.	Восьмьюстами	Девятьюстами
Prep.	О восьмистах	О девятистах

As you can see, the numerals 200, 300, 400, 500, 600, 700, 800, 900 include 2, 3, 4, 5, 6, 7, 8, 9 in itself, and have the same endings in hundred-part.

And finally, long numbers:

Thousand (1000) - **Тысяча** (singular)
Thousands (1000s) – **Тысячи** (plural)

Million (1.000.000) – **Миллион** (singular)
Millions – **Миллионы** (plural)

Billion (1.000.000.000) – **Миллиард** (singular)
Billions – **Миллиарды** (plural)

Trillion (1.000.000.000.000) – **Триллион** (singular)
Trillions – **Триллионы** (plural)

Nom.	**Тысяча - 1000**	**Тысячи – 1000 (pl)**
Gen.	Тысячи	Тысяч
Dat.	Тысячи	Тысячам
Acc.	Тысячу	Тысячи
Inst.	Тысячей	Тысячами
Prep.	О тысячи	О тысячах

Case	Singular	Plural
Nom.	**Миллион - million**	**Миллионы - millions**
Gen.	Миллиона	Миллионов
Dat.	Миллиону	Миллионам
Acc.	Миллион	Миллионы
Inst.	Миллионом	Миллионами
Prep.	О миллионе	О миллионах

Case	Singular	Plural
Nom.	**Миллиард - billion**	**Миллиарды - billions**
Gen.	Миллиарда	Миллиардов
Dat.	Миллиарду	Миллиардам
Acc.	Миллиард	Миллиарды
Inst.	Миллиардом	Миллиардами
Prep.	О миллиарде	О миллиардах

Case	Singular	Plural
Nom.	**Триллион - trillion**	**Триллионы - trillions**
Gen.	Триллиона	Триллионов
Dat.	Триллиону	Триллионам
Acc.	Триллион	Триллион
Inst.	Триллионом	Триллионами
Prep.	О триллионе	О триллионах

Declension of ordinal numbers

Ordinal numbers (first, second, third, fourth, fifth .... etc. up to infinity) are declined the **same as adjectives,** i.e. they have the same case endings. However, let's consider declension of one word:

Первый (m), Первая (f), Первое(n), Первые (pl) - First

Nom.	Перв<u>ый</u>(m)	Перв<u>ая</u>(f)	Перв<u>ое</u>(n)	Перв<u>ые</u>(pl)
Gen.	Перв<u>ого</u>	Перв<u>ой</u>	Перв<u>ого</u>	Перв<u>ых</u>
Dat.	Перв<u>ому</u>	Перв<u>ой</u>	Перв<u>ому</u>	Перв<u>ым</u>
Acc.	Перв<u>ый</u> / перв<u>ого</u>	Перв<u>ую</u>	Перв<u>ое</u>	Перв<u>ые</u> / перв<u>ых</u>
Inst.	Перв<u>ым</u>	Перв<u>ой</u>	Перв<u>ым</u>	Перв<u>ыми</u>
Prep.	О перв<u>ом</u>	О перв<u>ой</u>	О перв<u>ом</u>	О перв<u>ых</u>

All next ordinal numbers will have the same case endings. However, there is one complication here – Ordinal numbers can have unchanged part, as well as in English, pay attention to the underlined unchanged parts:

Втор**ой** – 2nd

Тр**е**тий – 3rd

Четв**ё**ртый – 4th

П**я**тый – 5th

Шест**ой** – 6th

Седьм**ой** – 7th

Восьм**ой** – 8th

Дев**я**тый – 9th

Дес**я**тый – 10th

Одиннадцатый – 11th

Двенадцатый – 12th

...

Двадцатый – 20th

Двадцать первый – 21th - twenty first

Двадцать второй – 22th

Тридцатый – 30th

Тридцать второй – 32th - thirty second

Сороковой – 40th

Пятидесятый – 50th

Шестидесятый – 60th

Семидесятый – 70th

Восьмидесятый – 80th

Девяностый – 90th

Сотый – 100th

Сто пятнадцатый – 115th – one hundred fifteenth

Сто двадцать седьмой – 127th – one hundred twenty seventh

Двухсотый – 200th

Тысячный – 1000th

Тысяча двухсотый – 1200th – one thousand two hundredth

Тысяча девятьсот девяносто пятый – 1995th – one thousand nine hundred ninety fifth (or nineteen ninety fifth if this is a year)

Двухтысячный – 2000th

Две тысячи семнадцатый – 2017th – two thousand seventeenth (or twenty seventeenth if this is a year)

Десятитысячный – 10000th

Стотысячный – 100000th

Миллионный – 1000000th

Миллиардный – 1000000000[th]

Триллионный – 1000000000000[th]

You can see that unchanged part of compound numbers is the same part as in English equivalent, that part doesn't get changed by gender and case. Let's decline one such compound number by cases:

2854th – две тысячи восемьсот пятьдесят четвёртый

Nom.		четвёртый
Gen.		четвёртого
Dat.	**Unchanged part**	четвёртому
Acc.	Две тысячи восемьсот пятьдесят	Четвёртый / четвёртого
Inst.		Четвёртым
Prep.		Четвёртом

You can use this online tool for checking declensions of numerals; just input a number there and it will show you all declensions of collective and ordinal numbers: http://numeralonline.ru/

Declension of nouns

A noun can belong to one of 3 declensions. These declensions determine case endings of nouns in each case. Here is how to define them:

DECLENSION I: feminine nouns ending in –А/-Я: БАБУШКА – grandma (feminine, ending -А), СЕМЬ**Я** – family (feminine, ending –Я)
And exceptional masculine nouns with "feminine" endings: ДЕДУШКА – granddad (masculine, ending -А), МУЖЧИН**А** – man (masculine, ending –А)

DECLENSION II: masculine nouns with zero endings, and neuter nouns ending in -О and -Е. For example, ДОМ - home (masculine, empty ending), КОНЬ – horse (masculine, empty ending), УТР**О** – morning (neuter, ending -О), СОЛНЦ**Е** – sun (neuter, ending -Е)

DECLENSION III: feminine nouns ending in -Ь. For example: НОЧ**Ь** – night, МЫШ**Ь** – mouse, КРОВАТ**Ь** – bed.

Let us consider the 6 words in singular and plural forms and look at their endings in each case:

КНИГА(feminine, 1ˢᵗ declension) – book, КНИГИ – books(plural)

Nominative	Книга	Книги
Genitive	Книги	Книг
Dative	Книге	Книгам
Accusative	Книгу	Книги
Instrumental	Книгой	Книгами
Prepositional	О книге	О книгах

ЗЕМЛЯ – land (feminine, 1st declension), ЗЕМЛИ – lands(plural)

Nom.	Земля	Земли
Gen.	Земли	Земель
Dat.	Земле	Землям
Acc.	Землю	Земли
Inst.	Землёй	Землями
Prep.	О земле	О землях

ПРОЕКТ – project (masculine, 2nd declension), ПРОЕКТЫ – projects(plural)

Nom.	Проект	Проекты
Gen.	Проекта	Проектов
Dat.	Проекту	Проектам
Acc.*	Проект	Проекты
Inst.	Проектом	Проектами
Prep.	О проекте	О проектах

ЗДАНИЕ – building (neuter, 2nd declension), ЗДАНИЯ – buildings (plural)

Nom.	Здание	Здания
Gen.	Здания	Зданий
Dat.	Зданию	Зданиям
Acc.*	Здание	Здания
Inst.	Зданием	Зданиями
Prep.	О здании	О зданиях

*- In the Declension II accusative case matches with nominative if the noun is **inanimate**, and when the noun is **animated**, accusative case matches with genitive. For example:

Nominative: Человек - human (animated), Стол – table (inanimate)

Accusative: Человека (animated, matches with genitive), Стол (inanimate, matches with nominative).

МЫСЛЬ – thought (feminine, 3rd declension), МЫСЛИ – thoughts

Nom.	Мысль	Мысли
Gen.	Мысли	Мыслей
Dat.	Мысли	Мыслям
Acc.	Мысль	Мысли
Inst.	Мыслью	Мыслями
Prep.	О мысли	О мыслях

СТЕПЬ – steppe (feminine, 3rd declension), СТЕПИ – steppes

Nom.	Степь	Степи
Gen.	Степи	Степей
Dat.	Степи	Степям
Acc.	Степь	Степи
Inst.	Степью	Степями
Prep.	О степи	О степях

Declension of adjectives and participles

Nouns differ by declensions, but adjective's case endings differ by hard and soft endings. Hard ones: ЫЙ, ОЙ, АЯ, ОЕ, ЫЕ and soft ones are ИЙ, ЯЯ, ЕЕ, ИЕ, i.e., those that contain the softening letter И. Let us consider two words in four variations (masculine, feminine, neuter, plural).

One with hard ending:

КРАСИВЫЙ (m), КРАСИВАЯ (f), КРАСИВОЕ (n), КРАСИВЫЕ (pl) — Beautiful

And one with soft ending:

СИНИЙ(m), СИНЯЯ(f), СИНЕЕ(n), СИНИЕ(pl) – blue

<u>Masculine:</u>

Nom.	Красивый	Синий
Gen.	Красивого	Синего
Dat.	Красивому	Синему
Acc.*	Красивый / красивого	Синий / Синего
Inst.	Красивым	Синим
Prep.	О красивом	О синем

*- if a masculine or plural adjective describes an **animated** object - accusative case will match with genitive, if **inanimated** – it will match with nominative case.

Feminine:

Nom.	Красивая	Синяя
Gen.	Красивой	Синей
Dat.	Красивой	Синей
Acc.	Красивую	Синюю
Inst.	Красивой	Синей
Prep.	О красивой	О синей

Neuter:

Nom.	Красивое	Синее
Gen.	Красивого	Синего
Dat.	Красивому	Синему
Acc.	Красивого	Синее
Inst.	Красивым	Синим
Prep.	О красивом	О синем

Plural:

Nom.	Красивые	Синие
Gen.	Красивых	Синих
Dat.	Красивым	Синим
Acc.	Красивые / Красивых	Синих / Синие
Inst.	Красивыми	Синими
Prep.	О красивых	О синих

Declension of participles

Participles have the same endings as adjectives, and case endings of participles and adjectives are the same. It is applied to all participles – active and passive, they all have the same endings:

Делающ**ий**(m), делающ**ая**(f), делающ**ее**(n), делающ**ие**(pl) – doing - active present tense participle

Играв**ий**(m), играв**шая**(f), играв**шее**(n), играв**шие**(pl) – playing - active past tense participle

Продаваем**ый**(m), продаваем**ая**(f), продаваем**ое**(n), продаваемые(pl) – being sold, passive present tense participle.

Сделанн**ый**(m), сделанн**ая**(f), сделанн**ое**(n), сделанные(pl) – made - passive past tense participle

And a participle formed from a reflexive verb:

The difference is only in postfix –СЯ that will be added in all declensions:

Строящийся(m), строящаяся(f), строящееся(n), строящиеся(pl) – building - present tense reflexive participle

Nom.	Делающ**ий**	Играв**ий**
Gen.	Делающ**его**	Играв**шего**
Dat.	Делающ**ему**	Играв**шему**
Acc.	Делающ**его** / Делающ**ий**	Играв**ий** / Играв**шего**
Inst.	Делающ**им**	Играв**шим**
Prep.	О делающ**ем**	О играв**шем**

Nom.	Продаваемый	Сделанный
Gen.	Продаваемого	Сделанного
Dat.	Продаваемому	Сделанному
Acc.	Продаваемый / продаваемого	Сделанный / сделанного
Inst.	Продаваемым	Сделанным
Prep.	О продаваемом	О сделанном

And for all participles (active, passive, present, past) formed from a reflexive verb, just add the postfix –СЯ:

Nom.	Строящийся
Gen.	Строящегося
Dat.	Строящемуся
Acc.	Строящийся / Строящегося
Inst.	Строящимся
Prep.	О строящемся

As you can see, participles are declined **the same way as adjectives.**

Use of cases

Case triggers are underlined by a <u>**bold line**</u>, declined words are underlined by a <u>thin line</u>.

Direct and indirect object

Read this chapter when you study the accusative and dative cases.

Direct object is an object of an action, the object upon which the action is performed.

Direct object is always in **Accusative case.**

For example:

Я <u>читаю</u> <u>книгу</u> – I read a book, *Книга - a book* is the direct object of the verb *Читать – to read.*

Я <u>люблю</u> <u>мороженное</u> – I love ice cream, *Мороженное – ice cream* is the direct object of the verb *Любить – to love.*

Indirect object is the object that receives an action of a verb.

Indirect object is always in **Dative case.**

Он <u>помогает</u> <u>другу</u> – He helps a friend. *Друг – friend* is indirect object of the verb *Помогать – to help,* because *the* friend is the receiver of the action "to help".

Он <u>объясняет</u> <u>нам</u> – He explains to us. *Мы – we (нас in dat. case)* is the indirect object of the verb *Объяснять.*

How to distinguish direct and indirect objects?

One verb can have both direct and indirect object, so one must be able to distinguish them. it is important to see the difference between Accusative and Dative cases.

Let's consider examples with direct and indirect objects with the verbs ДАВАТЬ – *to give* and ПОСЫЛАТЬ – *to send:*

Я <u>даю</u> <u>тебе</u> – I give (to) you – "теб**е**"(you) is in dative case

Я <u>даю</u> <u>тебя</u> – I give you (to) – "теб**я**"(you) is in accusative case

Я <u>посылаю</u> <u>моему сыну</u> сообщение – I send a message <u>to</u> my son – "моем**у** с**ы**ну" is in Dative case (I send <u>to whom?</u> – to my son)

Я <u>посылаю</u> <u>моего сына</u> в магазин – I send my son to the shop – мое**го** с**ы**на is in Accusative case (I send <u>whom?</u> – my son)

Also, a verb can have both indirect and direct objects in one sentence:

Он предлагает друзьям помощь – He offers help to the friends:

Друзья – friends is **indirect object** of the verb *Предлагать – to offer, because* it is receiver/beneficiary of the verb's action. It is declined in the Dative case;

Помощь – help is **direct object** of the verb *Предлагать – to offer,* it is declined in the Accusative case.

Президент дал обещания людям – The president gave promises to the people:

Обещания - promises is **direct object** of the verb *Дать – to give,* it is declined in the Accusative case;

Люди – people is **indirect object** of the verb *Дать – to give,* because it is receiver/beneficiary of the verb's action. It is declined in Dative case.

Transitive and intransitive verbs

There are verbs that can have a direct object, and there are verbs that don't or cannot.

Transitive verbs are verbs that can have a direct object, for example

Я читаю книгу – I read a book, where "книга – book" is declined in Accusative case, this is the direct object of the verb "читать – to read", the noun Книга is declined in Accusative case.

Intransitive verbs are verbs that cannot have a direct object. Instead they are accompanied by a preposition that require using a non-accusative case, or just require to use an appropriate case. By the way, all reflexive verbs are intransitive.

Он боится собак – He is afraid of dogs. The noun "собаки – dogs" is declined in Genitive case, this is **not** a direct object of the verb "бояться".

Also intransitive verbs can be accompanied by prepositions that require appropriate cases after them. For example:

Он договорился с другом – He reached an agreement with a friend. The verb "Договориться – to reach an agreement" is accompanied with the preposition "С – with" that require the Instrumental case after it.

In descriptions of Genitive and Instrumental cases you will find lists of intransitive verbs that require to use those cases.

Nominative case

Nominative case is initial form of a word (pronoun / noun / adjective / participle) without change. This case answers **the questions**:

Кто? – Who?

Что? – What?

When the Nominative case is used:

- **Это объект – This is an object**

<u>Это</u> <u>моя комната</u> – This is my room *(комната – room)*

<u>Это</u> <u>бутылка</u> – This is a bottle *(бутылка – bottle)*

- **Есть, был, была, были, было, будет, будут - There is/are/was/were/will be**

Здесь <u>есть</u> банком**ат** – <u>There is</u> an ATM here *(банкомат – ATM/cash machine)*

В нашем городе <u>будет</u> <u>новый аэропорт</u> – <u>There will be</u> a new airport in our city *(новый – new, аэропорт – airport)*

На поле <u>были</u> <u>цветы</u> – There were flowers in the field *(поле – field, цветы – flowers)*

- **In comparative after ЧЕМ – than**

Для меня физика интереснее <u>чем</u> <u>математика</u> – The physics is more interesting than mathematics for me *(физика – physics, математика – mathematics)*

Самолёт быстрее, <u>чем</u> <u>поезд</u> – An airplane is faster than a train *(самолёт – airplane, поезд – train)*

Genitive case

This is the most often used case in Russian language. It has the largest list of prepositions after which this case is used. Generally the Genitive case is used to express relation between two nouns.

Genitive case answers the questions:

Кого? – Whom?

Чего? – What?

Genitive case is used:

- **As analogue of English preposition "of"**

There is not the preposition "of" in Russian, instead one uses Genitive/Partitive case *(check the chapter "Partitive case")*

Дай мне пару <u>монет</u> – Give me a couple <u>of</u> coins *(пара – couple, монета – coin)*

Мы смотрели фотографии <u>красивого города</u> – We looked photos <u>of</u> a beautiful town (фотография – photo, красивый – beautiful, город – town/city)

Я искал в интернете слова <u>этой песни</u> – I was searching for the lyrics <u>of</u> this song in the internet (слова – lyrics, песня – song)

- **Possession**

Это дом <u>Сергея</u> – This is Sergey's home

Это машина <u>моего отца</u> – This is my father's car

- **At describing amount/quantity**

When we describe amount more than 1, we use genitive. There is a nuance: any quantity of items from 2 to 4 is declined as <u>singular</u>, and any quantity from 5 to 20 as <u>plural</u>. Also, from 22 to 24 – singular, from 25 to 30 – plural, and so on up to infinity.

Examples:

<u>Два</u> <u>яблока</u> – two apples (*яблоко – apple*)

<u>Три</u> <u>помидора</u> – three tomatoes (*помидор – tomato*)

<u>Четыре</u> <u>игрока</u> – four players (*игрок – player*)

<u>Пять</u> <u>посылок</u> – five parcels (*посылка – parcel*)

<u>Шесть</u> <u>слов</u> – six words (*слово – word*)

<u>Семь</u> <u>листов</u> – seven sheets (*лист – sheet*)

<u>Сто</u> <u>чашек</u> – one hundred cups (*чашка – cup*)

- **After МНОГО – much/many, МАЛО – little/few**

<u>У</u> <u>выпускников</u> есть много интересных возможностей – The graduates have many interesting opportunities (*выпускник – graduate, возможность*)

<u>У</u> <u>нас</u> осталось <u>много</u> вкусной е<u>ды</u> <u>после</u> праздника – We have many tasty food left after the celebration (*оставаться – to leave oneself, вкусный – tasty, еда – food, праздник – celebration*)

Почему в нашем коллективе так <u>мало</u> <u>молодых</u> <u>людей</u>? – Why there are so few young people in our collective? (*молодой – young, люди – people (always plural)*)

В этом музее <u>мало</u> <u>интересных</u> <u>экспонатов</u> – There are a few interesting showpieces in the museum (*экспонат – showpiece, музей – museum*)

- **After comparative <u>without</u> ЧЕМ – than**

Почему вторая часть книги <u>длиннее</u> <u>первой</u>? – Why the second part of the book is long<u>er</u> than the first one? *(часть – part, длинный – long, первый – first, второй – second)*

Деревянные дома <u>красивее</u> <u>кирпичных</u> – Wooden houses are more beautiful than brick ones *(красивый – beautiful, деревянный – wooden, кирпичный – brick (adjective))*

- **At describing lack of something**

У меня <u>нет</u> <u>подходящих деталей</u> для твоего велосипеда – I don't have appropriate parts for your bicycle *(деталь – detail/part, велосипед – bicycle, подходящий – appropriate)*

Здесь <u>нет</u> <u>железнодорожной станции</u> – There is not a railway station here *(железнодорожный – railway (adjective), станция – station)*

Думаю, что мне <u>не хватает</u> <u>витаминов</u> – I think that I have lack of vitamins *(думать – to think, не хватать – to have lack of - reflexive construction)*

- **When it is "Enough"**

Мне <u>хватает</u> <u>заработанных</u> <u>денег</u> – For me it is enough earned money *(хватать – to be enough, заработанный – earned, деньги – money (always plural))*

У нас есть <u>достаточно</u> <u>опыта</u> – We have enough experience *(достаточно – enough, опыт – experience)*

Не <u>достаточно</u> <u>времени</u> – Not enough time

- **After "У" in the construction "to have"**

У <u>нашего тренера</u> по танцам **очень большой опыт** – Our dance trainer has a big experience *(тренер – trainer, танцы – dances, очень – very)*

У <u>моих друзей</u> есть сво**я я**хта – My friends have own yacht *(яхта – yacht)*

У <u>наших соседей</u> есть собака – Our neighbors have a dog *(соседи – neighbors, собака – dog)*

- **In dates**

Read the chapter "Cases in dates".

- **After БОЛЕЕ – more**

Нам нужно <u>более</u> <u>двух помощников</u> – We need more than two helpers *(помощник – helper)*

На митинге было <u>более</u> <u>десяти тысяч человек</u> – There were more than ten thousand people in the rally *(человек – man/human/people, митинг – rally)*

- **After some verbs**

Imperfective / perfective - translation

Бояться / Побояться – to be afraid, to fear

Пугаться / Испугаться – to get scared

Касаться / Коснуться – to touch

Лишать / Лишить – to deprive

Лишаться / Лишиться – to lose

Придерживаться / Придержаться – to adhere, to follow

Избегать / Избежать – to avoid

Examples:

Почему ты <u>боишься</u> <u>пауков</u>? – Why are you afraid of spiders? *(паук – spider)*

Не <u>касайся</u> <u>оголённых проводов</u>! – Don't touch bare wires! *(оголённый – bare, провод – wire)*

Водителя <u>лишили</u> <u>водительских прав</u> – The driver was deprived of driving license *(водитель – driver, водительские права – driving license)*

Менеджер <u>лишился</u> <u>работы</u> – The manager has lost (his) job *(работа – job)*

Мы <u>придерживаемся</u> непопулярной точки зрения – We adhere to an unpopular point of view *(непопулярный – unpopular, точка зрения – point of view)*

Она всегда старается <u>избегать</u> <u>конфликтов</u> – She always tries to avoid conflicts (стараться – to try, всегда – always)

Prepositions that require Genitive case

Genitive case has the largest list of prepositions, so it requires a particular consideration.

Prepositions of directions

ИЗ – from, out of

ОТ – from, on

ИЗ-ПОД – from under

С, СО – from (notice, that this preposition also can mean *WITH* and be used with the instrumental case)

Examples:

Я е́ду из Москвы́ - I am going from Moscow (*е́хать – to go*)

Э́тот дом постро́ен из дорого́го де́рева – This house is built from an expensive tree (*постро́ен – built, дорого́й – expensive, де́рево – tree*)

Результа́т зави́сит от мно́гих фа́кторов – The result depends on many factors (*зави́сеть – to depend, мно́гий – many (adjective)*)

Мне ничего́ не ну́жно от тебя́ и твои́х друзе́й – I don't need anything from you and your friends (*друзья́ – friends*)

Он доста́л котёнка из-под маши́ны – He took a kitten from under the car (*котёнок – kitten, котёнка – kitten in accusative case*)

Убери́ коро́бки из-под крова́ти – Remove the boxes from under the bed

Возьми́ каранда́ш со стола́ – Take the pencil from the table (взять – to take, стол - table)

Мы **на**ча**л**и чи**та**ть <u>с</u> <u>пя**той**</u> <u>стра**ни**цы</u> – We started to read from fifth page

Connections in speech:

БЕЗ – without

ДЛЯ – for

ИЗ-ЗА – because of

КР**О**МЕ – apart from

ВВИД**У** – in the view of

ВМ**Е**СТО – instead of

НАСЧ**Ё**Т – about, as regards

ПОМ**И**МО – besides, apart from

ПОСР**Е**ДСТВОМ – through, by means of

ОТНОС**И**ТЕЛЬНО – regarding, in relation to, relatively

КАС**А**ТЕЛЬНО – concerning

ПР**О**ТИВ - against

Examples:

Нельз**я** перес**е**чь гран**и**цу <u>без</u> <u>паспорта</u> – One must not cross the border without passport (перес**е**чь – to cross, гран**и**ца – border)

Андр**е**й пришёл <u>без</u> <u>своей</u> <u>жен**ы**</u> – Andrey has come without his wife (жен**а** – wife)

Серёжа сд**е**лал под**а**рки <u>для</u> <u>б**а**бушки</u> <u>и</u> <u>д**е**душки</u> – Seryozha has made gifts for grandma and granddad (*бабушка – grandma, дедушка – granddad)*

Фото́граф купи́л но́вый объекти́в <u>для</u> <u>ста́рого</u> <u>фотоаппара́та</u> – The photographer has bought a new lens for the old photo camera *(объекти́в – lens, ста́рый – old, фотоаппара́т – photo camera)*

Мы не смогли́ пры́гнуть с парашю́том <u>из-за</u> <u>плохо́й</u> <u>пого́ды</u> – We could not jump with a parachute because of bad weather *(пры́гнуть – to jump, парашю́т – parachute, плохо́й – bad, пого́да – weather)*

Никто́ не пошёл на вечери́нку <u>кро́ме</u> <u>её подру́ги</u> – Nobody has gone to the party apart from her friend *(вечери́нка – party, подру́га – friend (female))*

<u>Ввиду́</u> но́вых ограниче́ний, мы не мо́жем сотру́дничать – In the view of the new restriction, we cannot collaborate *(ограниче́ние – restriction, сотру́дничать – to collaborate)*

Что ты ду́маешь <u>насчёт</u> <u>у́жина</u> в рестора́не? – What do you think about dinner in a restaurant? *(у́жин – dinner)*

Что ты уме́ешь гото́вить поми́мо су́па? – What can you cook besides soup? *(гото́вить – to cook, суп – soup)*

Мы мо́жем перевести́ вам де́ньги <u>посре́дством</u> <u>электро́нного перево́да</u> – We can transfer you money through electronic transfer *(перевести́ – to transfer, электро́нный – electronic, перево́д – transfer)*

<u>Относи́тельно</u> <u>Со́лнца</u>, Луна́ име́ет таку́ю же ско́рость, как Земля́ – Relatively to the Sun, the Moon has the same speed as Earth *(ско́рость – speed)*

<u>Каса́тельно</u> <u>на́шего про́шлого разгово́ра</u> .... – Concerning our last conversation ... *(про́шлый – last, разгово́р – conversation)*

Мы все <u>про́тив</u> <u>войны́</u> – We all are against war *(война́ – war)*

Positions in space:

У – at, near, from

ОКОЛО – near

ВОКР**У**Г – around

СРЕД**И** – among

ПОСРЕД**И** – midst, in the middle

СНАР**У**ЖИ – outside of

ВНЕ – beyond

ВНУТР**И** – inside, within

НАПР**О**ТИВ – in front of

Examples:

Я был на консультации **у** врач**а** – I have been at the doctor's consultation *(врач – doctor)*

Спрос**и**те **у** м**е**неджер**а** – Ask (from) the manager

Я в**и**дел ег**о у** тог**о** д**о**м**а** – I saw him near that house (тот – that)

Мы припарков**а**ли маш**и**ну <u>около</u> <u>кирпичного здания</u> – We have parked the car near the brick building *(кирп**и**чный – brick (adjective), зд**а**ние – building)*

Ты в**и**дел н**о**вый торг**о**вый центр <u>около</u> <u>центрального парка</u>? – Have you seen the new trade center near the central park? *(торг**о**вый центр – trade center, центр**а**льный – central)*

<u>Посред**и**</u> <u>больш**о**й пл**о**щади</u> установ**и**ли п**а**мятник – One installed a monument in the middle of the big square *(больш**а**я пл**о**щадь – big square, установ**и**ть – to install, п**а**мятник - топитепт)*

<u>Посреди</u> <u>солнечного дня</u> внезапно пошёл дождь – Suddenly it rained in the middle of the sunny day *(идёт дождь – it rains, солнечный – sunny)*

Этот коврик крепится <u>снаружи туристического рюкзака</u> – This mat is attached outside of the touristic backpack *(коврик – mat, туристический – touristic, рюкзак – backpack)*

Почему мусорное ведро находится <u>снаружи</u> <u>магазина</u> – Why is the bin located outside of the store? *(мусорное ведро – bin, магазин – store)*

Молодёжь <u>вне</u> <u>политики</u> – The youth is beyond the politics (молодёжь – youth, политика – politics)

Эта проблема <u>вне</u> <u>наших интересов</u> – This problem is beyond our interests *(интерес – interest)*

Вы были <u>внутри</u> <u>горной пещеры</u>? – Have you been inside the mountain cave? *(горный – mountain (adjective), пещера – cave)*

<u>Внутри</u> <u>этого фрукта</u> есть косточка – There is a stone inside this fruit *(косточка – stone, фрукт – fruit)*

Она будет нас ждать <u>напротив</u> <u>театра</u> – She will wait for us in front of theater *(ждать – to wait, театр – theatre)*

<u>Напротив</u> <u>нашей школы</u> открылся магазин – in front of our school one opened a store *(школа – school, магазин – store)*

Movement:

ВДОЛЬ – along

МИМО – (pass) by

ВНУТРЬ – (to) inside

ВНИЗ – down

ВВЕРХ – to the top

Examples:

Авт**о**бус **е**дет по дор**о**ге <u>вдоль</u> <u>рек**и**</u> – The bus goes by the road along the river *(автобус – bus, ехать – to go (by vehicle), дорога – road, река – river)*

Мы д**о**лго шли <u>вдоль</u> <u>дл**и**нного заб**о**ра</u> – We were going along the fence for long time *(долго – long time, длинный – long, забор – fence)*

Глеб прош**ё**л <u>м**и**мо</u> <u>поворо**т**а</u> – Gleb has passed by the turn (поворо**т** – turn)

Мы про**е**хали <u>м**и**мо</u> <u>изв**е**стного муз**е**я</u> – We have passed by the cinema *(проехать – to pass (by vehicle), известный – famous, музей – museum)*

Дав**а**й зайд**ё**м <u>внутрь</u> <u>**э**того забр**о**шенного зд**а**ния</u> – Let's come inside this abandoned building *(заброшенный – abandoned, здание – building)*

Полож**и** это <u>внутрь</u> <u>своег**о** кошельк**а**</u> – Put it inside your wallet *(положить – to put, кошелёк – wallet)*

Orientation in space:

СПЕРЕД**И** (ОТ) – in front, in front of

ВПЕРЕД**И** – in front, in front of

СЛ**Е**ВА (ОТ) – left of

СПР**А**ВА (ОТ) – right of

СЗ**А**ДИ (ОТ) – behind

СВ**Е**РХУ (ОТ) – above/over, in the top of

СН**И**ЗУ (ОТ) – below, from below

ВНИЗ**У** – in the bottom of

Examples:

<u>Спереди от</u> автобуса едет грузовик – A truck is going in front of the bus *(грузовик – truck)*

Ты видишь, кто идёт <u>спереди от него</u>? – Can you see who is going in front of him?

<u>Впереди</u> меня в очереди много людей – There are many people in front of me in the queue

Солдаты шли <u>впереди</u> танковой колонны – The soldiers were going in font of the tank column *(танковый – tank (adjective), column – колонна)*

Вход в аптеку находится <u>слева от</u> чёрной двери – The entrance to the pharmacy is to the left of the black door *(чёрный – black, дверь – door)*

Маленький куст растёт <u>слева от</u> высокого дерева – A small bush grows to the left of the high tree *(маленький – small, куст – bush, расти – to grow, высокий – high, дерево – tree)*

Я стою <u>справа от фонтана</u> – I stand to the right of fountain *(фонтан – fountain)*

Наш офис находится <u>справа от</u> выхода из лифта – Our office is located to the right of the exit from the lift *(офис – office, выход – exit, лифт – lift)*

<u>Сзади</u> твоей головы летает комар – A mosquito is flying behind your head *(голова – head, летать – to fly, комар – mosquito)*

<u>Сзади от</u> красного кабриолета стоял микроавтобус – A minibus was behind the red cabriolet *(красный – red, стоять – to stand/to be, микроавтобус – minibus)*

<u>Сверху</u> <u>страницы</u> написано название книги – The book's title is written in the top <u>of</u> the page *(страница – page, написан – written, название – title, книга – book)*

Стая птиц пролетела <u>сверху</u> <u>соснового леса</u> – Flock <u>of</u> birds has flown above the pine forest *(стая – flock, птица – bird, пролететь – to fly, сосновый – pine (adjective), лес – forest)*

<u>Снизу</u> <u>высокой горы</u> не было видно верхушки <u>из-за облаков</u> – One could not see the peak of the high mountain from below because of the clouds *(высокий – high, видно – seen, гора – mountain, верхушка – peak, облако – cloud)*

<u>Снизу</u> <u>высокого дерева</u> опадает кора – the crust fall off from below the high tree *(дерево – tree, опадать – to fall off, кора – crust)*

Посмотри, не лежит ли эта книга <u>внизу</u> <u>стеллажа</u> – Look whether this book lies in the bottom of shelving *(книга – book, лежать – to lie down)*

<u>Внизу</u> <u>страницы</u> есть партнёрская ссылка – There is a partner link in the bottom of the page *(ссылка – link)*

Time:

ВО ВРЕМЯ – during

В ТЕЧЕНИЕ – during, for, within (in the sense of time)

ПОСЛЕ – after

ДО – before, until, till

ОКОЛО – about

С, СО - since

Examples:

<u>Во время</u> футбольного матча мы пили пиво – We drank beer during the football match (пиво – beer, пить – to drink, футбольный – football (adjective), матч – match)

<u>Во время</u> холодной погоды мы были дома – We were home during the bad weather *(холодный – cold, погода – weather, дома – at home)*

<u>В течение</u> долгого времени* она не могла найти работу – She could not find a job for long time (долгий – long, время – time)

*-Время has exceptional form in the genitive case – ВРЕМЕНИ.

<u>В течение</u> многих лет* мы ездили на море летом – We went to the sea at summer for many years (многий – many (adjective), море – sea, лето – summer)

*Лет is exceptional genitive form of the word ГОДЫ – years (plural). Singular form is regular. It is also the genitive form of ЛЕТА – summers (plural).

<u>После</u> Нового Года мы продолжим учиться – We will continue to study after the New Year (новый – new, год – year, продолжить – to continue, учиться – to study)

<u>После</u> обеденного перерыва я Вам помогу - I will help you after lunch break *(обеденный перерыв – lunch break, помочь – to help)*

Ты можешь мне это объяснить <u>до</u> начала лекции? – Can you explain it to me before the beginning of the lecture? *(объяснить – to explain, начало – beginning, лекция – lecture)*

Вы должны написать отчёт <u>до</u> <u>сегодняшнего вечера</u> – You must write the report before today's evening (написать – to write, отчёт – report, сегодняшний вечер – today's evening)

Это займёт <u>около</u> <u>трёх часов</u> – It will take about three hours *(занять – to take (time), час – hour)*

Вам придётся* подождать <u>около</u> <u>двух дней</u> – You will have to wait about two days *(прийтись* – to have to)*

*- read more about this form of "to have to" in the chapter "Dative case"

<u>Со времени</u> <u>правления</u> этого президента многое изменилось – Since the time of board <u>of</u> this president many things got changed *(правление – board, многое – many things, измениться – to get changed)*

<u>С</u> того момента мы стали друзьями – Since that moment we became friends *(стать – to become, друг – friend)*

Dative case

Dative case indicates the recipient or beneficiary of the verb's action – i.e. this case is applied only to an indirect object – recipient of the action, to which the action is directed or a beneficiary for whom the action is done. This case is used to describe giving, sending, direction of an action.

Answers the questions:

Кому? – To whom?

Чему? – To what?

Before learning more about this case, read the chapter "Direct and indirect object".

Dative case is applied to an indirect object of a verb. The verbs that describe giving to someone/something or an action directed to someone/something.

Hint phrase "I give it (to whom?) <u>to you</u>"

This is the list of most often used verbs that can have an indirect object, i.e. an object that requires use of Dative case:

(imperfective / perfective):

Дава́ть / дать – to give

Дари́ть / подари́ть – to give (a gift)

Посыла́ть / посла́ть – to send

Отправля́ть / отпра́вить – to send

Ве́рить / пове́рить – to believe

Предлага́ть / предложи́ть– to offer

Говори́ть / сказа́ть – to say , to tell

Рассказывать / рассказать – to tell

Помогать / помочь – to help

Звонить / позвонить – to call (by phone)

Мешать / помешать – to disturb

Обещать / пообещать – to promise

Объяснять / объяснить – to explain

Examples:

<u>Расскажи</u> <u>всем нам</u>, куда ты ездил – Tell us all where did you go (*все – all, куда – whereto*)

Почему ты не <u>веришь</u> <u>этим людям</u>? – Why you don't believe these people? (*люди – people*)

<u>Кому</u> я должен <u>отправить</u> письмо? – To whom do I have to send the letter? (*письмо – letter*)

Что мы <u>подарим</u> <u>нашему тренеру</u> на день рождения? – What will we give to our trainer for (his) birthday?

Also, the Dative case is used:

- **After prepositions:**

К – to
ПО – by, on

Examples:

Пошли <u>к</u> <u>моей сестре</u>! – Let's go to my sister! (*сестра – sister*)

Поехали <u>к</u> <u>нашим родителям</u> в гости – Let's go on a visit to our parents (*родители – parents, в гости – on a visit*)

Не стучи <u>по</u> <u>столу</u>! – Don't knock on the table (*стучать – knock, стол – table*)

Не ходи <u>по</u> <u>мокрому полу</u>! – Don't walk on the wet floor (*ходить – to walk, мокрый – wet, пол – floor*)

- **Subject of the verbs НРАВИТЬСЯ – to like (to be pleased by), КАЗАТЬСЯ – to seem, ХОТЕТЬСЯ – to want.**

Мне нравится – I like *(мне – subject of the verb нравиться)*

Моему коту нравится пить молоко – My cat likes to drink milk *(кот – cat, молоко – milk)*

Учителю в школе кажется, что мы плохо учимся – It seems to the teacher in the school that we study bad *(учитель – teacher, школа – school, плохо – bad, учиться – to study)*

Кому ещё кажется, что я не прав? – To whom more it seems, that I am not right? (прав – right)

Твоим детям тоже хочется пойти с нами? – Does your children want to go with us too? *(дети – children, тоже – too)*

Директору не хочется поднимать зарплаты – The director doesn't want to raise salaries *(поднимать – to raise, зарплата – salary)*

- **With construction НУЖЕН / НУЖНА / НУЖНО / НУЖНЫ – need**

Новому предприятию нужны молодые специалисты – The new enterprise needs young specialists *(предприятие – enterprise, молодой – young)*

Талантливому фотографу нужны модели для фотосессий – A talented photographer needs models for photo session *(талантливый talented, фотосессия – photo session)*

- **Construction "to me it is …"**

<u>Мне</u> <u>холодно</u> – I feel cold (literally – "to me it is cold")

<u>Нам</u> <u>жарко</u> – We feel hot (literally – "to us it is hot")

<u>Туристам</u> б**ы**ло <u>интер**е**сно</u> – Tourists were interested (literally – "it was interesting to tourists)

Здесь <u>всем</u> <u>понр**а**вилось</u> – Everyone liked it here *(literally – "to everyone it was liked here")*

- **Благодар**я **– thanks to / due to**

<u>Благодар**я**</u> <u>мо**е**му отцу</u>, я получ**и**л хор**о**шее образов**а**ние – Thanks to my father, I've obtained a good education *(от**е**ц – father, образов**а**ние – education)*

<u>Благодар**я**</u> нед**а**вним соб**ы**тиям, экон**о**мика улучш**а**ется – Due to the recent events, the economy gets better *(нед**а**вний – recent, соб**ы**тие – event, улучш**а**ться – to get better)*

- **Приход**иться **– one more form of "to have to"**

Present	Past	Future
Прих**о**дится	Приход**и**лось (imp.) Пришл**о**сь (perf.)	Прид**ё**тся (only perf.)

<u>Доктор**а**м</u> в больн**и**це <u>прих**о**дится</u> мн**о**го раб**о**тать – Doctors in the hospital have to work a lot

<u>Пассаж**и**рам</u> <u>пришл**о**сь</u> ждать зад**е**рживающийся рейс – The passengers had to wait for the delaying flight (пассаж**и**р – passenger, зад**е**рживающийся – delaying, рейс – flight)

<u>Студ**е**нтам</u> <u>прид**ё**тся</u> мн**о**го уч**и**ться – The students will have to study a lot

- **According to ...**

There are several ways to say "according to .." in Russian, and some of them are accompanied with prepositions that determine a case. However, these two aren't accompanied by a preposition and require dative case after them:

СОГЛАСНО ... – according to ...

СЛЕДУЯ ... - according to ...

Examples:

<u>Согласно</u> <u>правилам</u>, это запрещено – According to the rules, it is forbidden *(правило – rule, запрещено – forbidden)*

<u>Согласно</u> <u>известному тезису</u> – According to the famous thesis *(известный – famous, тезис – thesis)*

<u>Следуя</u> <u>закону</u>, это наказуемо – According to the law, it is punishable *(закон – law, наказуемо – punishable)*

<u>Следуя</u> <u>данному тексту</u>, проблем нет вообще – According to this text, there are not problems at all *(вообще – at all)*

Accusative case

This case indicates a direct object of an action – i.e. an object upon which the action of the verb is performed.

Pay attention at the endings of masculine and plural endings in this case (jump to the chapter "case endings of nouns", "case endings of adjectives")

Read the chapter "Direct and indirect object" before learning more about this case.

Accusative case is applied to the object of an action, e.g. "I want an object, I can see the object, I wait an object, I buy an object"

Я крашу стену – I am painting the wall (красить – to paint, стена – wall)

Строители строят большой торговый центр – The builders are building a big trade center (*строитель – builder, большой – big, торговый центр – trade center*)

Я хочу купить дешёвый телефон – I want to buy a cheap phone (*купить – to buy, дешёвый – cheap*)

Они слушают музыку – They listen to music (*слушать – to listen*)

Ты видишь того человека? – Can you see that man? (*видеть – to see, человек – man, human*)

Accusative case is also used with these prepositions::

В – into, to
НА – onto, to
ЗА – for
ЧЕРЕЗ – through, across
ПРО - about

Examples:

Положи яблоко в холодильник – Put the apple into the refrigerator *(положить – to put, яблоко – apple, холодильник – refrigerator)*

Давай сходим в театр – Let's go to the theater (театр – theater)

Положи книгу на полку – Put the book onto the shelve *(книга – book, полка – shelve)*

Я иду на тренировку – I am going to the workout *(тренировка – workout)*

Мы болеем за футбольную команду – We support the football team *(болеть за – to support (a sport team), команда – team)*

Люди голосуют за оппозиционного кандидата – People vote for the opposition candidate *(голосовать – to vote, оппозиционный – opposition)*

Мы должны пройти через трудности – We have to pass through difficulties (трудности – difficulties)

Этот поезд не едет через Москву – This train doesn't go through Moscow

В газете была статья про шахтёров – There was an article about miners in the newspaper

Нам рассказали про предстоящую работу – We were told about coming work

Instrumental case

This case is called "Instrumental" because it is used to indicate an instrument/tool or means of completing an action.

Answers the questions **Кем?** - By whom? **Чем?** – by what?/By which means?

When it is used:

- **Analogue of English "by" in the sense "something is done <u>by</u> the object"**

Как отвернуть гайку <u>гаечным ключом</u>? – How to unscrew the nut <u>by</u> the spanner? *(отвернуть – to unscrew, nut – гайка, spanner – гаечный ключ)*

Этот текст написан <u>синей ручкой</u> – This text is written <u>by</u> the blue pen *(написан – write, синий – blue, ручка – pen)*

Сделай это <u>своими руками</u> – Make it by your hands *(рука – hand, arm)*

Художник рисует картину <u>кистью</u> – Artist draws a picture <u>by</u> a brush *(художник – brush, рисовать – to draw, кисть – brush)*

Трава покрыта <u>снегом</u> – The grass is covered by snow *(трава – grass, покрыть – to cover, снег – snow)*

- **With prepositions**

С (СО) – with
РЯДОМ С – next to, near
МЕЖДУ – between
НАД – above, over
ПОД - under
ЗА – after (in the sense of following an object), behind

Examples

Дети гуляют <u>с родителями</u> – The children walk with parents (дети – children, гулять – to walk/stroll, родители – parents)

Мы шли <u>с тяжёлыми рюкзаками</u> – We were going with heavy backpacks (*тяжёлый – heavy, рюкзак – backpack*)

Мой офис находится <u>рядом со станцией метро</u>* - My office is located near the metro station (офис – office, станция метро – metro station)

*-Exception: word "метро" is not declined by cases.

Дерево растёт <u>рядом с дорогой</u> – A tree grows next to the road (*дерево – tree, расти – to grow, дорога – road*)

<u>Между</u> теми высокими горами есть дорога – There is a road between those high mountains (*высокий – high, гора – mountain*)

<u>Между</u> двумя домами есть улица – There is a street between two houses (дом – house, улица – street)

Самолёт летит <u>над океаном и островами</u> – The airplane is flying above the ocean and the islands (*самолёт – airplane, лететь – to fly, океан – ocean, остров – island*)

Картина висит на стене <u>над часами</u> – The picture hangs on the wall above the watch (*картина – picture, висеть – to hang, часы - watch*)

Метро находится <u>под землёй</u> – The metro is located under the ground (*земля – ground*)

Коробка лежит <u>под диваном</u> – The box lies under the couch (*коробка – box, лежать – to lie, диван – couch*)

Кот бежит за собакой – A cat is running after a dog *(кот – cat, бежать – to run, собака – dog)*

Белка прячется за зелёным кустом – The squirrel is hiding behind the green bush *(белка – squirrel, прятаться – to hide, зелёный – green, куст – bush)*

- **After "I want to be ...; I was ...; I will be ...; I would be ..." but NOT "I am ..."**

Толя хочет быть инженером – Tolya wants to be an engineer *(инженер – engineer)*

Он был хорошим доктором – He was a good doctor

Выпускники нашего университета будут дипломированными специалистами – The graduates of our university will be certified specialists *(выпускник – graduate, университет – university, дипломированный – certified)*

Если бы я был американцем, я бы учил русский язык – if I were an American, I would learn the Russian language *(американец – American)*

- **After "work as ...", "serve as ..."**

Пётр работает программистом – Pyotr works as a programmer *(работать – to work)*

Анна работает учительницей – Anna works as a teacher *(учительница – teacher (female))*

Он служит в армии солдатом – He serves in army as a soldier *(армия – army, солдат – soldier)*

- **After СТАТЬ – to become**

Паша хочет стать космонавтом – Pasha wants to become an astronaut *(космонавт – astronaut)*

Когда ты <u>стал</u> <u>таким худым</u>? – When did you become so slim? *(такой – so/such, худой – slim)*

Когда он <u>станет</u> <u>умным</u>? – When he become smart? *(умный – smart)*

- **Являться – to be**

This form of "to be" is used to emphasize meaning.

Он <u>является</u> <u>директором</u> этой компании – He is the director of this company

Кто <u>является</u> <u>его</u> <u>родственником</u>? – Who is his relative?

- **Заниматься – to be engaged in, to do, to practice**

<u>Каким спортом</u> ты <u>занимаешься</u>? – What kind of sport do you do?

Она <u>занимается</u> <u>бальными танцами</u> – She is engaged in ballroom dances

- **In seasons (in winter, in sprint, in autumn, in summer)**

ЛЕТО – summer, <u>ЛЕТОМ</u> – in summer

ОСЕНЬ – autumn, <u>ОСЕНЬЮ</u> – in autumn

ЗИМА – winter, <u>ЗИМОЙ</u> – in winter

ВЕСНА – spring, <u>ВЕСНОЙ</u> – in spring

Also, an adjective or a pronoun with seasons, for example:

СЛЕДУЮЩИМ ЛЕТОМ – (in) next summer

ПРОШЛОЙ ОСЕНЬЮ – (in) last autumn

ЭТОЙ ЗИМОЙ – (in) this winter

ТОЙ ВЕСНОЙ – (in) that spring

Examples:

Мы поедем на море <u>летом</u> – We will go to the sea in summer (лето – summer)

Учёба начинается <u>осенью</u> – The studies begin in autumn (*начинаться – to begin, осень - autumn*)

<u>Зимой</u> будет холодно – It will be cold in winter (*зима – winter, холодно – cold*)

Я хочу начать <u>заниматься спортом</u> весн<u>ой</u> – I want to start to do sport in spring (*начать – to start, заниматься спортом – to do sport*)

- **In the morning, day, evening, night**

УТРОМ – in the morning (утро – morning)

ДНЁМ – in the afternoon (день – day)

ВЕЧЕРОМ – in the evening, tonight (вечер – evening)

НОЧЬЮ – at night (ночь – night)

Examples:

Что будем делать <u>утром</u>? – What will we do in the morning?

Увидимся завтра <u>вечером</u> – See you tomorrow evening (*увидимся – see you, завтра – tomorrow*)

Где ты будешь <u>днём</u>? – Where will you be in the afternoon?

Я напишу тебе <u>ночью</u> – I will write to you at night

- ## Other verbs that require Instrumental case after them

Гордиться – to be proud of

Делиться поделиться – to share

Питаться – to eat/to feed upon

Пользоваться / воспользоваться – to use

Наслаждаться / насладиться – to enjoy

Любоваться / полюбоваться – to admire

Восхищаться / восхититься – to admire/ to marvel

Увлекаться / увлечься– to be addicted

Управлять – to control, to drive, to manage, to govern

Руководить – to run, to manage

Командовать – to command

Рисковать – to risk

Казаться – to seem

Владеть – to own, to know

Болеть / заболеть – to be ill

Examples:

Мы не <u>гордимся</u> <u>своими достижениями</u> – We are not proud of our achievements *(достижение – achievement)*

Мой друг <u>поделился</u> <u>конфетами</u> – My friend shared sweets *(конфеты – sweets)*

<u>Чем</u> <u>питается</u> хомяк? – What feeds on a hamster? (literally: "what a hamster is fed by?") *(хомяк – hamster)*

Какими медицинскими препаратами вы **пользуетесь?** – Which medical products do you use? *(медицинский препарат – medical product)*

Она наслаждается жизнью – She enjoys life *(жизнь – life)*

Посетители любуются картинами – The visitors admire the pictures *(посетитель – visitor, картина – picture)*

Родители восхищаются достижением своего **сы**на – The parents admire the achievement of their son *(родители- parents, достижение – achievement, сын – son)*

Мой брат увлекается компьютерными играми – My brother is addicted to computer games *(компьютерная игра – computer game)*

Менеджер управляет коммерческим отделом – A manager manages a sales department *(коммерческий отдел – sales department)*

Предприниматель руководит крупной компанией – An entrepreneur manages a large company *(предприниматель – entrepreneur, крупный - large)*

Генерал командовал армией – The general commanded the army

Бизнесмен рисковал большой суммой денег – A businessman risked big amount of many *(бизнесмен - businessman, сумма – amount)*

Эта задача кажется лёгкой – This task seems easy *(задача – task, лёгкий – easy)*

Кто владеет этим домом? – Who owns this house? (дом – house)

Чем они болеют? – What they are sick of?

Prepositional (Locative) case

Designates an object of speech or a place of an object. This case is always used with prepositions:

О, ОБ – about
НА – on
В – in
Answers the questions:
О ком? – about whom?
О чём? – about what?
Где? – where? (Locative case)

Examples:

Расскажи мне о твоём путешествии – Tell me about your travel *(рассказать – to tell, путешествие – travel)*

На уроке истории нам рассказывали о великой октябрьской революции – In the history class we were told about the great October revolution *(урок – class, история – history, великий – great)*

Что это у тебя на голове? – What is on your head? *(голова – head)*

На вершине горы очень красиво – It is very beautiful on the peak of the mountain *(вершина – peak, очень - very)*

В хорошем учебнике должно быть много примеров – There must be many examples in a good textbook *(учебник – textbook, пример – example)*

В холодильнике должна быть еда – There must be food in the refrigerator *(холодильник – refrigerator, еда – food)*

*- Read the next chapter "Locative case 2" in order to understand the difference between Prepositional and Locative.

Also

Locative case 2

This case is usually not separated from Prepositional. However Prepositional and Locative are different cases, but their rules are similar and usually they match.

> Locative case indicates a location of an abject. It answers the question Где? – Where? And always used with prepositions:
> НА – on
> В – on
> Answers the question Где? – where?

Same as Prepositional, excepting some preposition (О, ОБ) that are added to the Prepositional case.

The easy thing is that only **some masculine nouns** have a Locative form, and they all have the ending **–У**. Here they are:

<u>На</u> <u>носу</u> – on the nose

<u>На</u> <u>шкафу</u> – on the cupboard

<u>На</u> <u>мосту</u> – on the bridge

<u>В</u> аэропорту – in the airport

<u>На</u> <u>полу</u> – on the floor

<u>На</u> <u>посту</u> – it the post

And here is the difference between Locative and Prepositional case for these nouns:

<u>О</u> <u>носе</u> – about nose (Prepositional)

<u>На</u> <u>носу</u> – on the nose (Locative)

<u>Об</u> аэропорте – about airport (Prepositional)

<u>В</u> аэропорту – in the airport (Locative)

Vocative case

This case is widely used in other Slavic Languages, but in Russian just a little.

Vocative case is used for identification an addressed person.

Primarily the vocative case is used when one calls a person by name, for example "John!" or "Kate!" etc. Not all names have vocative form. Let's learn how to know if a name has a vocative form:

Names ending in –Я will have Я changed to Ь:

Ан**я** (nom.) - Ан**ь**! (voc.) – Anya, female name

Сен**я** (nom.) – Сень! (voc.) – Senya, male name

Жен**я** (nom.) – Жень! (voc.) – Zhenya, male/female name

Тол**я** (nom.) – Тол**ь**! (voc.) – Tolya, male name

Наст**я** (nom.) – Наст**ь**! (voc.) – Nastya, female name

Ол**я** (nom.) – Ол**ь**! (voc.) – Olya, female name

And others.

Names ending in –A will have zero ending:

Серёж**а** (nom.) – Серёж! (voc.) - Seryozha, male name

Нин**а** (nom.) – Нин! (voc.) – Nina, female name

Зин**а** (nom.) – Зин! (voc.) – Zina, female name

Ир**а** (nom.) – Ир! (voc.) – Ira, female name

Лен**а** (nom.) – Лен! (voc.) – Lena, female name

Саш**а** (nom.) – Саш! (voc.) – Sasha, female name

And others.

Names with zero ending don't have vocative form (i.e. vocative form matches with nominative):

Андр**ей** (nom.) – Андр**ей**! (voc.) – Andrey, male name

Вад**им** (nom.) – Вад**им**! (voc.) – Vadim, male name

The types of names considered above are types of Russian names. A non-Russian name can have vocative form only if it has the same ending as a Russian one. Other non-Russian names don't have vocative forms.

Also, not only names can be declined in Vocative case:

Мама (nom.) – Мам! (voc.) – Mom

Папа (nom.) – Пап! (voc.) – Dad

Partitive case

This case is used when we need to indicate a part or share of an uncountable item. Partitive case can be used with *some* instead of Accusative, and it has the same endings as Genitive. Also, the Partitive case can be used with nouns instead of English preposition "of", as well as Genitive, but it almost always matches with Genitive, there are only some words that have own Partitive form – you will find them in this chapter.

When we use Partitive case with a verb – this case indicates a direct object, like Accusative.

Partitive case is used with the verbs:

Хот**е**ть – to want

Тр**е**бовать – to require

Жел**а**ть – to wish

Прос**и**ть – to ask

Иск**а**ть – to look for

Examples:

Я хочу пив<u>о</u> – I want beer (Accusative) – it means what I want a beer, one of beers, any beer – one of many items.

Я хочу пив<u>а</u> – I want some beer (Partitive) – it means that I want some beer, as a part/share of uncountable item "beer".

Преподав**а**тель тр**е**бует внима́ни<u>е</u> – The professor requires attention (Accusative)

Преподав**а**тель тр**е**бует внима́ни<u>я</u> – The professor requires attention (Partitive)

Он**и** пр**о**сят д**е**ньги – They ask for money (Accusative)

Они просят денег – They ask for some money (Partitive)

Желать счастье – To wish happiness (Accusative)

Желать счастья – To wish happiness (Partitive)

Искать смысл – To look for a sense (Accusative)

Искать смысла – To look for sense (Partitive)

Partitive case with nouns and words that have own Partitive form:

Сахар – sugar (Nominative)

Ложка сахара – spoon of sugar (Genitive)

Ложка сахару – spoon of sugar (Partitive)

Песок – sand/sugar (Nominative)

Стакан песка – glass of sand/sugar (Genitive)

Стакан песку – glass of sand/sugar (Partitive)

Чай – tea

Чашка чая – cup of tea(Accusative)

Чашка чаю – cup of tea (Partitive)

Чеснок – garlic

Головка чеснока – head of garlic (Genitive)

Головка чесноку – head of garlic (Partitive)

Waitative case

This case is used with the verb ЖДАТЬ – *to wait* and similar verbs by sense, e.g. ОЖИДАТЬ – *to expect/to wait*, ДОЖИДАТЬСЯ – *to wait*

After these verbs we use the Accusative case, however sometimes we also can use the Waitative. The form of Waitative case always matches with Genitive, so there are not special endings:

Я жду письм**о** – I wait for a letter (Accusative)

Я жду письм**а** – I wait for a letter (Waitative)

Мы ожид**а**ем п**о**езд – We are waiting for train (Accusative)

Мы ожид**а**ем п**о**езд**а** – We are waiting for train (Waitative)

Translative case

This case indicates transition from one state to another. Translative case always matches either the instrumental case or the plural nominative depending on way of use.

There are two ways of use:

- **To run for/To be going to become – Translative case matches with plural nominative**

Баллотироваться в <u>президенты</u> – To run for president

Выбрать в <u>руководители</u> – To elect to be a chief

Идти в <u>актёры</u> – To be going to become an actor

Идти в <u>космонавты</u> – To be going to become an astronaut

- **To change a state of a verb's object from one to another – Translative case matches with Instrumental**

Мы сделаем Америку <u>великой</u> снова! – We will make America great again! *(motto of Donald Trump)*:
Verb – сделать (to make), its object – Америка, its new state – великая (great)

Опыт сделает тебя <u>востребованным специалистом</u> – Experience will make you an in-demand specialist *(востребованный – in-demand)*:
Verb - сделать (to make), its object – ты, its new state – востребованный специалист (in-demand specialist)

Давай сделаем обложку книги <u>красивой</u> – Let's make the book cover beautiful *(обложка – cover)*:
Verb - сделать (to make), its object – обложка книги (book cover), its new state – красивая (beautiful)

Cases in dates

The Russian format of a date is DD.MM.YYYY (DAY.MONTH. YEAR)

First of all, memorize that a date consists of ordinal numbers (those numbers that in English end in –th)

And there are some complications in case use in dates:

Look at this format: DD.MM.YYYY

DD* is in Nominative/Genitive case

MM is in Genitive case (this is not a numeral)

YYYY is in Genitive case.

*- *When we say a date itself – we say DD in nominative case, when we say about something happening in this date, we use DD in genitive case*

Let's consider the date 29th January 1992 (25.01.1992).

In Russian it will literally have such form: "twenty fifth of November of one thousand nine hundred ninety second year"-

Двадцать пятое(25th) января (of January) тысяча девятьсот девяносто второго (of 1992th) года (year).

And when we talk about something happening on this date, as it was mentioned above, we use DD in genitive case:

Это произошло двадцать пятого января тысяча девятьсот девяносто второго года – It happened 29th January 1992.

Exercises

Define declension of each noun (I, II or III):

1. Стена – wall ____

2. Площадь – square ____

3. Пиво – beer ____

4. Гитара – guitar ____

5. Кухня – kitchen ____

6. Картина – picture ____

7. Окно – window ____

8. Стекло – glass ____

9. Чашка – cup ____

10. Сталь – chair ____

11. Поезд – train ____

12. Танец – dance ____

13. Музыка – music ____

14. Хомяк – hamster ____

15. Пианино – piano ____

16. Ночь – night ____

17. Стол – table ____

18. Университет – university ____

19. Звезда – star ____

20. Поле – field ____

Also, decline these 20 nouns by cases, in singular as well as plural variant.

Decline pronouns by appropriate cases:

21. Что _____ нужно? – (ТЫ – you) What do you(singular) need?

22. Здесь нет _____ ключей – (ТВОЙ – your) There are not your keys here

23. Кто тебе сказал о _____ планах? – (МОЙ – my) Who told you about our plans?

24. Ты слышишь _____? – (ОНА – she) Do you hear her?

25. У нас в магазине нет _____ продукта – (ТАКОЙ – such) We don't have such product in the store

26. Ты встретил _____ из наших друзей? – (КТО-НИБУДЬ – someone) Did you meet anyone of our friends?

27. ____ нравится бегать – (ОНИ – they) They like to run

28. Почему она не пригласила _____? (НИКТО – no one) – Why didn't she invite anyone?

29. Ты пригласишь _____ на танец? (Я – I) – Will you invite me to a dance?

30. Магазин находится за _____ зданием (ЭТО – this) – The store is located behind this building

31. Где вы забыли _____ багаж? (ВАШ – yours) – Where did you forget your luggage?

32. _____ вы хотели пригласить в гости? (КТО – who) – Whom did you want to invite on a visit?

33. _____ сайтом ты пользуешься для изучения Русского языка? (КАКОЙ – which) – Which site do you use for learning the Russian language?

34. Мы любим _____ собаку (НАШ – our) – We love our dog

35. _____ программами ты пользуешься? (КАКОЙ – which) – Which programs do you use?

36. У тебя есть _____ поесть? (ЧТО-НИБУДЬ – something) – Do you have something to eat?

37. Что вы будете делать со _____ вещами? (СВОЙ – own, your) – What will you do with your things?

38. Ты _____ спросил? (ВСЕ – everyone) – Have you asked everyone?

39. Вы знаете _____ здесь? (КТО-ЛИБО – anyone) – Do you know anyone here?

40. Зачем _____ нужны cars? (ВСЕ – everybody) – Why do everybody need cars?

Decline words by appropriate cases:

41. Первый день _____ был очень интересным (НАШЕ ПУТЕШЕСТВИЕ – our travel) – The first day of our travel was very interesting

42. Из окна _____ была видна Красная Площадь (НАШ ОТЕЛЬ– our hotel) – The Red Square was seen from the window of our hotel

43. Мы гуляли в _____ (КРАСИВЫЙ ПАРК – beautiful park) – We walked in a beautiful park

44. Я учусь на факультете _____ (МЕЖДУНАРОДНЫЕ ОТНОШЕНИЯ – international relations) – I study in the faculty of international relations

45. Они обедали в _____ (ДОРОГОЙ РЕСТОРАН – expensive restaurant) – They had a lunch in an expensive restaurant

46. Наш университет организует много мероприятий для _____ (СТУДЕНТЫ – students) – Our university organizes many events for students

47. Москва была _____ в нашем путешествии по России (ПЕРВЫЙ ГОРОД – first city) – Moscow was the first city in our travel around Russia

48. Ты можешь показать мне Петербург на _____ (КАРТА МИРА – world map) – Can you show me Petersburg in the world map?

49. В Нью-Йорке живут люди _____ (ВСЕ НАЦИОНАЛЬНОСТИ – all nationalities) – There are people of all nationalities living in New-York

50. Не бросайте _____ здесь (МУСОР – rubbish) – Don't throw rubbish here

51. Жизнь в _____ дешевле, чем в _____ (ПЕТЕРБУРГ – Petersburg, МОСКВА – Moscow) – Life in Petersburg is cheaper than in Moscow

52. Президент рассказал об _____ (ЭКОНОМИЧЕСКИЙ ПРИОРИТЕТ – economic priority) – The president has told about the economic priority

53. Согласно _____, нельзя курить в общественных местах (ЗАКОН – law) – According to the law, one must now smoke in public places

54. На жёстком диске не достаточно _____ (ПАМЯТЬ – memory) – It is not enough memory in the hard drive

55. Попроси брата купить две _____ воды (БУТЫЛКА – bottle) – Ask (your) brother to buy two bottles of water

56. Сергей выучил много _____ (ИНОСТРАННЫЙ ЯЗЫК – foreign language) – Sergey has learnt many foreign languages

57. Мы бежали к _____ (BUS STOP – АВТОБУСНАЯ ОСТАНОВКА) – We were running to the bus station

58. Ты будешь встречать _____ (ГОСТИ – guests) – You will meet guests

59. Прогресс _____ и _____ сделал нашу жизнь гораздо комфортнее (НАУКА – science, ТЕХНИКА – technics) – The progress of science and technics has made our life much more comfortable

60. Часть Луны освещена _____ (СОЛНЕЧНЫЙ СВЕТ – sunlight) – Part of Moon is lightened by the sunlight

61. Благодаря _____ _____, удалось изобрести новое лекарство (УСИЛИЯ – efforts, СПЕЦИАЛИСТЫ – specialists) – Due to efforts of specialists, one managed to invent a new medicine

62. Задачи, поставленные перед _____, были сложными (УЧЁНЫЕ – scientists) – The tasks set for scientists were difficult

63. Лауреаты _____ - очень умные люди (Нобелевская премия – Nobel Prize) – The laureates of the Nobel Prize are very smart people

64. В эксперименте участвовали триста (300) _____ (ШКОЛЬНИК – schoolboy) – 300 schoolboys participated in the experiment

65. Количество _____ на _____ увеличилось на двадцать процентов (ПОСЕТИТЕЛИ – visitors, САЙТ – website) – Amount of visitors in the website was increased by twenty percent

66. Вчера на море волны были очень _____ (ВЫСОКИЙ – high) - The waves in the sea were very high yesterday

67. Инженер работает с _____ (КОМРЬЮТЕРЫ – computers) – The engineer works with computers

68. Фабрика производит _____ (КАЧЕСТВЕННЫЕ ПРОДУКТЫ – qualitative products) – The factory produces qualitative products

69. В Русском языке есть три _____ _____ (СКЛОНЕНИЕ – declension, СУЩЕСТВИТЕЛЬНЫЕ – nouns) – There are three declensions of nouns in Russian language

70. Ты встречал _____ в Сибири? (МЕДВЕДИ – bears) – Did you meet bears in Siberia?

71. Вы принимаете _____ (РУССКИЕ РУБЛИ – Russian roubles) – Do you accept Russian roubles?

72. Завтра я пойду к _____ (ВРАЧ – doctor) – Tomorrow I will go to a doctor

73. Ты читала какой-нибудь _____ о _____ (БЛОГ – blog, ПУТЕШЕСТВИЯ – travels) – Have you read any travel blog? (literally: blog about travels)

74. Я отдам велосипед на ремонт в _____ (ВЕЛОМАСТЕРСКАЯ – bike workshop) – I will give (my) bicycle for repair to the bike workshop

75. Священник будет служить в _____ (ЦЕРКОВЬ – church) – The priest will serve in the church

76. Вы будете готовиться к _____ (ЭКЗАМЕН – exam) – Will you prepare for exam?

77. Директор встретился со _____ (СВОИ КОЛЛЕГИ – his/own colleagues) – The director have met with his colleagues

78. Почему вы едите так много _____ (ЯБЛОКИ – apples) – Why do you eat so many apples?

79. Закрой _____ пожалуйста (ДВЕРЬ – door) – Close the door please

80. На этой улице был _____ (ХОРОШИЙ РЕСТОРАН – good restaurant) – There was a good restaurant in this street

81. **Если** бы ты был кандидатом в президенты, что бы ты пообещал _____ (НАРОД – people) – If you were a presidential candidate, what would you promise to the people?

82. Когда ты ходил к _____? (СТОМАТОЛОГ – dentist) – When did you go to a dentist?

83. Роман был написан _____ (ИЗВЕСТНЫЙ ПИСАТЕЛЬ – famous writer) – The novel was written by a famous writer

84. Вадим работает _____ (ЖУРНАЛИСТ – journalist) – Vadim works as a journalist

85. Мы гуляли по _____ (ПАРК – park) – We walked around park

86. Эту бумагу нужно резать _____ (НОЖНИЦЫ – scissors) – One must cut this paper by scissors

87. Он ходит в _____ каждый день (СПОРТЗАЛ – gym) – He goes to gym everyday

88. Вы помните советы _____? (ВАШИ РОДИТЕЛИ – your parents) – Do you remember advices of your parents?

89. Женя курит восемь _____ в день (СИГАРЕТА – cigarette) – Zhenya smokes eight cigarettes per day

90. Ребёнок залез на _____ (КРЫША – roof) – A child climbed on a roof

91. Адвокат занимается _____ (ЮРИДИЧЕСКИЕ ВОПРОСЫ – legal issues) – An attorney is engaged in legal issues

92. Что это? – Это _____ (ВЕРТОЛЁТ – helicopter) – What is this? This is helicopter

93. Она голосует за _____ (ДЕМОКРАТИЧЕСКАЯ ПАРТИЯ – democratic party) – She votes for democratic party

94. Государство регулирует _____ (ЧАСТНОЕ ПРЕДПРИНИМАТЕЛЬСТВО – private entrepreneurship) – The state regulates private entrepreneurship

95. В _____ этого языка это слово имеет разные значения (РАЗНЫЕ ДИАЛЕКТЫ – different dialects)

96. Согласно _____, та территория нейтральна (МЕЖДУНАРОДНЫЙ ДОГОВОР – international treaty) – According to the international treaty, that territory is neutral

97. Что произошло в _____ вчера? (СОЕДИНЁННЫЕ ШТАТЫ АМЕРИКИ – USA) – What happened in the United States of America yesterday?

98. Рынок _____ сейчас очень большой (МИНИ-ЭЛЕКТРОСТАНЦИЯ – mini-power plant) – The market of mini power plants is very now.

99. Вчера мы ночевали в _____ (ДЕШЁВЫЙ КЕМПИНГ – cheap camping) – Yesterday we spend the night in a cheap camping

100. В соответствии с _____ _____, участники получат финансовую поддержку (ПРОГРАММА – program, РАЗВИТИЕ ПРЕДПРИНИМАТЕЛЬСТВА – development of entrepreneurship) – In accordance with the program of development of entrepreneurship, the participants will get financial support

101. Мне не нужны _____! (ВАШИ СОВЕТЫ – your advices) – I don't need your advices!

102. Моя дочь мечтает стать _____ _____ (УЧИТЕЛЬНИЦА – teacher, АНГЛИЙСКИЙ ЯЗЫК – English language) – My daughter is dreaming to become an English language teacher (<u>Teacher of English Language</u>)

103. Когда здесь будет _____ (СЛЕДУЮЩИЙ ФЕСТИВАЛЬ – next festival) – When there will be the next festival here?

104. Вам достаточно _____ в _____? (СОЛЬ – salt, СУП – soup) – Is it enough salt for you in the soup?

105. Твоя сумка лежит под _____ (СТОЛ – table) – Your bag is under the table

106. _____ легче выучить иностранный язык, чем _____ человеку (РЕБЁНОК – child, ВЗРОСЛЫЙ – adult) – For a child it is easier to learn a foreign language than for an adult man.

107. Можешь помочь мне решить _____ (ЭТА ЗАДАЧА – this task) – Can you help me to solve this task?

108. _____ люди плавают в _____ (ЛЕТО – summer, ОЗЕРО – lake) – At summer people swim in the lake.

109. Использование _____ (СВАРОЧНЫЙ АППАРАТ – Welding machine) – Use of welding machine

110. Ты видел, кто идёт сзади от _____ (ТЫ – you) – Have you seen who is going behind you?

111. Ты пойдёшь домой после _____ (ВЕЧЕРИНКА – party) – Will you go home after party?

112. У тебя есть _____ (МЕЧТА – dream) – Do you have a dream?

113. Куда мы пойдём завтра _____ (УТРО – morning) – Where will we go tomorrow morning?

114. Сколько раз ты делал _____ во время _____ (ПРИСЕДАНИЯ – sit-ups, ТРЕНИРОВКА – workout) – How many times did you do sit-ups during the workout?

115. Учёба в школе начинается _____ (ПЕРВЫЙ – first, СЕНТЯБРЬ – September) – The studies in school begin in 1st September (1.09).

116. Вы читали _____ (РУССКАЯ КЛАССИЧЕСКАЯ ЛИТЕРАТУРА – Russian classic literature) – Did you read Russian classic literature?

117. Его компьютер заражён _____ (ВИРУС – virus) – His computer is infected with a virus

118. Напиши текст _____ (БОЛЬШОЙ ШРИФТ – big font) – Write the text by a big font

119. Давай прыгнем с _____ (ПАРАШЮТ – parachute) – Let's jump with parachute

120. Не забудь покормить _____ (ХОМЯК – hamster) – Don't forget to feed the hamster

121. Что можно приготовить из этих _____ (ИНГРЕДИЕНТЫ – ingredients) – What one can prepare from these ingredients?

122. Прочитайте _____ внимательно (ИНСТРУКЦИЯ – instruction) – Read the instruction carefully

123. _____ понравилось это мероприятие (ВСЕ УЧАСТНИКИ – all participants) – All participants liked this event

124. Наш автобус будет ехать вдоль _____ _____ (НАБЕРЕЖНАЯ – quay, РЕКА – river) – Will our bus travel along the quay of the river?

125. Мотоцикл быстрее _____
(ВЕЛОСИПЕД – bicycle) – Motorcycle is faster than a bicycle

126. У вас в меню есть какие-нибудь _____ кроме _____ (БЛЮДА – dishes, МЯСНЫЕ – meat (adjective)) – Do you have any dishes apart from meat ones in the menu?

127. _____ пришлось согласиться с _____ _____ (СТУДЕНТЫ – students, РЕЗУЛЬТАТЫ – results, ЭКЗАМЕН – exam) – Students had to agree with exam results (<u>with results of exam</u>)

128. _____ пришлось ждать в аэропорту (ПАССАЖИРЫ – passengers) – Passengers had to wait in the airport

129. Что _____ нужно от _____? (ВЫ – you, ОНИ – they) – What do you need from them?

130. Антон путешествует на _____ по _____ _____ (ПОЕЗД – train, ВСЯ СТРАНА – whole country) – Anton travels by train around the whole country

131. _____ работает твоя _____? (КТО – who, СЕСТРА – sister) – As who does your sister work?

132. Я ждал тебя десять _____ (МИНУТЫ – minutes) – I was waiting for you for 10 minutes

133. _____ он Вам является? (КТО – who) Who is he to you?

134. _____ _____ ты занимаешься? (КАКОЙ СПОРТ – which sport) – Which sport are you engaged in?

135. Сейчас около _____ _____ (СЕМЬ – seven, ЧАСЫ – hours) – It is about 7 o'clock now (literally: now it is about 7 hours)

136. Благодаря _____ _____,
я получил _____ _____
(ХОРОШЕЕ ОБРАЗОВАНИЕ – good education,
ХОРОШАЯ РАБОТА – good job) – Thanks to the good
education, I got a good job

137. Куда ты поедешь _____ _____
(СЛЕДУЮЩАЯ ЗИМА – next winter) – Where will you
go next winter?

138. Разработчики создали _____ _____
_____ (НОВАЯ КОМПЬЮТЕРНАЯ ИГРА – new
computer game) – Developers created a new computer
game

139. Я бы хотела быть _____ - (МОЛОДАЯ –
young) - I wish I were young (female)

140. Положи деньги на _____ (МОЯ
ТУМБОЧКА – my bedside table) – Put the money onto
my bedside table

141. Давай сделаем наш отпуск _____
(НЕЗАБЫВАЕМЫЙ – unforgettable) – Let's make our
vacation unforgettable

142. _____ выставки было скучно (ВСЕ
ПОСЕТИТЕЛИ – all visitors) – All visitors of the
exhibition felt boring (It was boring for all visitors of
the exhibition)

143. Из-за _____? (ЧТО – what) – Because of
what?

144. _____ ты хочешь стать, когда будешь
_____ (КТО – who, ВЗРОСЛЫЙ – adult) –
Whom do you want to become when you are an adult?

145. _____ нравится гулять под _____ без
_____(ТЫ – you, ДОЖДЬ – rain, ЗОНТИК
- umbrella) – Do you like to walk in the rain without an
umbrella? (literally: walk under the rain)

146. В магазине много _____ со _____
(ТОВАРЫ – goods, СКИДКИ – discounts) – There are many goods with discounts in the store

147. Ленинградское шоссе является _____
_____ _____ в _____
(САМАЯ ЗАГРУЖЕННАЯ ДОРОГА – the most loaded road, РОССИЯ - Russia) – Leningradskoye highway is the most loaded road in Russia

148. Об _____ _____ писали в
_____(ЭТО СОБЫТИЕ – this event, ГАЗЕТА - newspaper) – It was written about this event in a newspaper

149. Обменный курс зависит от _____
_____(МНОГИЕ ФАКТОРЫ – many factors) – Exchange rate depends on many factors

150. Оксана не пользуется _____
_____, она водит _____
_____ (ОБЩЕСТВЕННЫЙ ТРАНСПОРТ – public transport, СВОЯ МАШИНА – own car) – Oksana doesn't use public transport, she drives own car

151. Активисты отправили письмо _____
(ПРЕЗИДЕНТ – president) – The activists have sent a letter to the president

152. _____ _____ требуется наличие команды (КАЖДЫЙ КАНДИДАТ – each candidate) – Each candidate needs a command

153. Сколько _____ _____ нужно?
(ДОКАЗАТЕЛЬСТВО – proof, ВЫ – you) – How many proofs do you need?

154. Сколько _____ ты посетил за _____
_____ (СТРАНЫ – countries, ПРОШЛЫЙ ГОД – last year) – How many countries did you visit for the last year?

155. Ты **е**здил куда-нибудь _____
_____ (ПРОШЛОЕ ЛЕТО – last summer) – Did you go anywhere last summer?

156. Я ув**е**рен, что В**а**ня б**у**дет _____
_____ (ХОР**О**ШИЙ ОТ**Е**Ц - good father) – I am sure that Vanya will be a good father

157. На _____ **у**чится К**о**ля в _____
(КТО – who, КОЛЛ**Е**ДЖ – college) – What does Kolya study in the college? (literally: what does Kolya study to be ....)

158. Нам не хват**а**ет _____ на ур**о**ках
_____ (МУЖЧ**И**НЫ – men, Т**А**НЦЫ – dances) – We have lack of men in dance classes

159. Рестор**а**н предлаг**а**ет _____ на
_____по _____ (СК**И**ДКА – discount, ВСЁ МЕН**Ю** – whole menu, П**Я**ТНИЦЫ – Fridays) – The restaurants offers a discount for the whole menu in Fridays

160. От**е**ц горд**и**тся _____ (СВО**И**
Д**Е**ТИ – own children) – The father is proud by own children

161. Расск**а**жите нам о сво**и**х _____ от
_____ (ВПЕЧАТЛ**Е**НИЯ – impressions, СПЕКТ**А**КЛЬ – spectacle) – Tell us about your impressions from the spectacle

162. Уч**а**стие в семин**а**ре явл**я**ется
_____ (БЕСПЛ**А**ТНЫЙ – free) – Participation in the seminar is free

163. _____ _____ она над**е**нет
сег**о**дня? (КАК**А**Я ОД**Е**ЖДА – what (kind of) clothes) – What kind of clothes will she wear today?

164. Первая часть **этой** книги интереснее
_____ и _____ (ВТОРАЯ – second,
ТРЕТЬЯ – third) – The first part of this book is more
interesting than the second and the third one

165. Аня гуляла со _____ (СВО**Я** СОБАКА –
own(her) dog) – Anya walked with her dog

166. Как заработать на _____ в
_____ (ПРОДАЖИ – sales, ИНТЕРН**Е**Т -
internet) – How to make money on sales in the
internet?

167. Деятельность в **о**бласти _____
_____ (ИНФОРМАЦИ**О**ННЫЕ
ТЕХНОЛ**О**ГИИ – information technologies) – Activities
in the field of information technologies

168. Изучи**т**е _____ _____
_____ чтобы продвиг**а**ть ваш
_____ (СТАТ**И**СТИКА – statistics,
ПОИСКОВ**Ы**Е ЗАПР**О**СЫ – queries, САЙТ – website) –
Research the statistics of search queries in order to
promote your website

169. _____ _____ нужн**а**
_____ (КАЖДЫЙ ТОВАР – each product,
РЕКЛАМА – advertisement) – Each product needs an
advertisement

170. Сколько сто**и**т ар**е**нда _____
_____ в _____
(МАЛЕНЬКИЙ **О**ФИС – small office, БИЗНЕС-ЦЕНТР
– business center) – How much is the rent of a small
office in the business center?

171. Что вчер**а** показывали по _____
(ТЕЛЕВ**И**ЗОР – TV) – What was shown yesterday in the
TV?

172. Вы боитесь _____? (МЕДВЕДИ – bears) – Are you afraid of bears?

173. Какая камера самая лучшая для записи _____ (ВИДЕОБЛОГ – video blog) – Which camera is the best for video blog recording?

174. Не беги за _____ (Я – I) – Don't run after me!

175. Во время _____, отношения между _____ и _____ были очень _____ (ХОЛОДНАЯ ВОЙНА – cold war, СОВЕТСКИЙ СОЮЗ – Soviet Union, АМЕРИКА – America, НАПРЯЖЁННЫЕ – tense) – The relations between Soviet Union and America were very tense during the cold war

176. Чтобы не ошибиться с _____ _____ _____, проконсультируйтесь с _____ (ВЫБОР – selection, ТЕМА – subject, ДИПЛОМНАЯ РАБОТА – graduate work, ПРЕПОДАВАТЕЛЬ – professor) – In order not to be mistaken with subject selection for the graduate work, consult with the professor

177. Нам нужно определить _____ _____ _____ (ЦЕНА – price, НАШ ПРОДУКТ – our product) – We need to determine price or our product

178. Работая с _____, не забывайте о _____ (КЛИЕНТЫ – clients, ВЕЖЛИВОСТЬ – politeness) – Working with clients, don't forget about politeness

179. Парашютисты покидают _____ на _____ четыре тысячи метров (САМОЛЁТ – airplane, ВЫСОТА – altitude) – Parachute jumpers leave airplane in the altitude of 4000 meters

180. Кирилл и Настя хотят поехать на поезде через _____ (ВСЯ РОССИЯ – whole Russia) – Kirill and Nastya want to go by train across the whole Russia

181. Папа придёт домой поздно _____ (НОЧЬ – night) – Dad will come home at late night

182. Вы бы хотели сделать ваше хобби _____ _____ (СВОЯ ПРОФЕССИЯ – own profession?) – Would you like to make your hobby own profession?

183. Вы доверяете _____ (ПРАВИТЕЛЬСТВО – government) – Do you trust the government?

184. Что вы думаете об _____ в _____ (ИНВЕСТИРОВАНИЕ – investing, КРИПТОВАЛЮТА – crypto currency) – What do you think about investing to crypto currency?

185. Что вы думаете насчёт _____ в _____ _____ (РАБОТА – work, КРУПНАЯ КОМПАНИЯ – large company) – What do you think about work in a large company?

186. Этот праздник посвящён _____ в _____ (ВЕЛИКОЕ СОБЫТИЕ – great event, ИСТОРИЯ - history) – This holiday is dedicated to a great event in the history

187. Ты пользуешься _____ (ДЕЗОДОРАНТ – deodorant) – Do you use a deodorant?

188. У _____ в _____ есть прибор для _____ _____ (ПИЛОТ – pilot, КАБИНА – cockpit, ИЗМЕРЕНИЕ – measurement, ВЫСОТА – altitude) – A pilot has an altitude measurement device in the cockpit

189. _____ в _____ было _____ (УТРО – morning, ХРАМ – church, БОГОСЛУЖЕНИЕ – divine service) – There was a divine service in the church at morning

190. Что находится внутри _____ (ЭТА КОРОБКА – this box) – What is inside this box?

191. Андрей работал _____ на _____ (МАШИНИСТ – train driver, ЖЕЛЕЗНАЯ ДОРОГА - railroad) – Andrey worked as a train driver in the railroad

192. Ты почистил _____? (КОМНАТА – room) – Have you cleaned the room?

193. Мы пойдём к _____ в гости? (НАШИ РОДСТВЕННИКИ – our relatives) – Will we go to our relatives on a visit?

194. Зачем ограничивать доступ к _____ _____ (СОЦИАЛЬНЫЕ СЕТИ – social networks) – Why to restrict access to social networks?

195. В _____ был открыт _____ _____ (МОСКВА – Moscow, НОВЫЙ ПАРК – new park) – A new park was opened in Moscow

196. Зачем _____ нужно идти к _____? (БАБУШКА – grandma, ВРАЧ – doctor) – Why the grandma needs to go to doctor?

197. _____ пришлось писать _____ (ВСЕ СОТРУДНИКИ – all fellow workers, ОТЧЁТ - report) – All fellow workers had to write a report

198. Протестующие собирались на _____ вокруг _____ (ПЛОЩАДЬ – square, ПАМЯТНИК – monument) – Protestors gathered in the square around the monument

199. Из-за _____ _____ не разрешили перейти _____? (ЧТО – what, ОНИ – they, ГРАНИЦА – border) – Because of what they were not allowed to cross the border?

200. Что вы _____ можете предложить для решения _____ _____? (МЫ – we, ЭТА СЛОЖНАЯ ЗАДАЧА – this difficult task) – What can you offer us for solving this difficult task?

Answers

1. 1
2. 3
3. 2
4. 1
5. 1
6. 1
7. 2
8. 2
9. 1
10. 3
11. 2
12. 2
13. 1
14. 2
15. 2
16. 3
17. 2
18. 2
19. 1
20. 2
21. Тебе, dat.
22. Твоих, gen.
23. Моих, prep.
24. Её, acc.
25. Такого, gen.
26. Кого-нибудь, acc.
27. Им, dat.
28. Никого, acc.
29. Меня, acc.
30. Этим, inst.
31. Ваш, acc.

32. Кого, acc.

33. Каким, inst.

34. Нашу, acc.

35. Какими, inst.

36. Что-нибудь, nom.

37. Своими, inst.

38. Всех, acc.

39. Кого-либо, acc.

40. Всем, dat.

41. Нашего путешествия, gen.

42. Нашего отеля, gen.

43. Красивом парке, prep.

44. Международных отношений, gen.

45. Дорогом ресторане, prep.

46. Студентов, gen.

47. Первым городом, prep.

48. Карте мира, prep.

49. Всех национальностей, gen.

50. Мусор, acc.

51. Петербурге, prep.; Москве – prep.

52. Экономическом приоритете – prep.

53. Закону, dat.

54. Памяти, gen.

55. Бутылки, gen.

56. Иностранных языков, gen.

57. Автобусной остановке, dat.

58. Гостей, acc.

59. Науки, gen.; Техники, gen.;

60. Солнечным светом, inst.

61. Усилиям, dat.; Специалистов, gen.
62. Учёными, inst.
63. Нобелевской премии, gen.
64. Школьников, gen.
65. Посетителей, gen.; Сайт, prep.
66. Высокими, inst.
67. Компьютерами, inst.
68. Качественные продукты, acc.
69. Склонения, gen.; Существительных, gen.
70. Медведей, acc.
71. Русские рубли, acc.
72. Врачу, dat.
73. Блог, acc.; Путешествиях, inst.
74. Веломастерскую, acc.
75. Церкви, prep.
76. Экзамену, dat.
77. Своими коллегами, inst.
78. Яблок, gen.
79. Дверь, acc.
80. Хороший ресторан, nom.
81. Народу, dat.
82. Стоматологу, dat.
83. Известным писателем, inst.
84. Журналистом, inst.
85. Парку, dat.
86. Ножницами, inst.
87. Спортзал, acc.
88. Ваших родителей, gen.
89. Сигарет, gen.

90. Кр**ы**шу, acc.

91. Юрид**и**ческими вопр**о**сами, inst.

92. Вертол**ё**т, nom.

93. Демокр**а**т**и**ческую п**а**ртию, acc.

94. Ч**а**стное предприним**а**тельство, acc.

95. Р**а**зных диал**е**ктах, prep.

96. Междунар**о**дному догов**о**ру, dat.

97. Соедин**ё**нных шт**а**тах Ам**е**рики, prep.

98. М**и**ни-электрост**а**нций, gen.

99. Деш**ё**вом к**е**мпинге, prep.

100. Прогр**а**ммой, inst.; Разв**и**тия предприним**а**тельства, gen.

101. В**а**ши сов**е**ты, nom.

102. **У**тром, inst.

103. Сл**е**дующий фестив**а**ль, nom.

104. С**о**ли, gen.; С**у**пе, prep.

105. Стол**о**м, inst.

106. Взр**о**слому, dat.; Реб**ё**нку, dat.

107. **Э**ту зад**а**чу, acc.

108. Л**е**том, inst.; **О**зере, prep.

109. Св**а**рочного аппар**а**та, gen.

110. Теб**я**, gen.

111. Вечер**и**нки, gen.

112. Мечт**а**, nom.

113. **У**тром, inst.

114. Присед**а**ния, acc.; Тренир**о**вки, gen.

115. П**е**рвого, gen.; Сентябр**я**, gen.

116. Р**у**сскую класс**и**ческую литерат**у**ру, acc.

117. В**и**русом, inst.

118. Большим шрифтом, inst.
119. Парашютом, inst.
120. Хомяка, acc.
121. Ингредиентов, gen.
122. Инструкцию, acc.
123. Всем участникам, dat.
124. Набережной, gen.; Реки, gen.
125. Велосипеда, gen.
126. Блюда, nom.; Мясных, gen.
127. Студентам, dat.; Результатами, inst.; Экзамена, gen.
128. Пассажирам, dat.
129. Вам, dat.; Них, gen.
130. Поезде, prep.; Всей стране, dat.
131. Кем, inst.; Сестра, nom.
132. Минут, gen.
133. Кем, inst.
134. Каким спортом, inst.
135. Семи, gen.; Часов, gen.
136. Хорошему образованию, dat.; Хорошую работу, acc.
137. Следующей зимой, inst.
138. Новую компьютерную игру, acc.
139. Молодой, inst.
140. Мою тумбочку, acc.
141. Незабываемым, inst.
142. Всем посетителям, dat.
143. Чего, gen.
144. Кем, inst.; Взрослым, inst.

145. Тебе, dat.; Дождём, inst.; Зонтика, gen.;

146. Товаров, gen.; Скидками, inst.

147. Самой загруженной дорогой, inst.; России, prep.

148. Этом событии, prep.; Газете, prep.;

149. Многих факторов, prep.

150. Общественным транспортом, inst.; Свою машину, acc.

151. Президенту, dat.

152. Каждому кандидату, dat.

153. Доказательств, gen.; Вам, dat.

154. Стран, gen.; Прошлый год, acc.

155. Прошлым летом, inst.

156. Хорошим отцом, inst.

157. Кого, acc.; Колледже, prep.

158. Мужчин, gen.; Танцев, gen.

159. Скидки, acc.; Всё меню, acc.; Пятницам, dat.

160. Своими детьми, inst.

161. Впечатлениях, prep.; Спектакля, gen.

162. Бесплатным, inst.

163. Какую одежду, acc.

164. Второй, gen.; Третьей, gen.

165. Своей собакой, inst.

166. Продажах, prep.; Интернете, prep.

167. Информационных технологий, gen.

168. Статистику, acc.; Поисковых запросов, gen.; Сайт, nom.

169. Каждому товару, dat.; Реклама, nom.

170. Маленького офиса, gen.; Бизнес-центре, prep.

171. Телевизору, dat.

172. Медведей, gen.
173. Видеоблога, gen.
174. Мной, inst.
175. Холодной войны, gen.; Советским союзом, inst.; Америкой, inst.; Напряжёнными, inst.
176. Выбором, inst.; Темы, gen.; Дипломной работы, gen.; Преподавателем, inst.
177. Цену, acc.; Нашего продукта, gen.
178. Клиентами, inst.; Вежливости, prep.
179. Самолёт, acc.; Высоте, prep.
180. Всю Россию, acc.
181. Ночью, inst.
182. Своей профессией, inst.
183. Правительству, dat.
184. Инвестировании, prep.; Криптовалюту, acc.
185. Работы, gen.; Крупной компании, prep.
186. Великому событию, dat.; Истории, prep.
187. Дезодорантом, inst.
188. Пилота, inst.; Кабине, prep.; Измерения, gen.; Высоты, gen.
189. Утром, inst.; Храме, prep.; Богослужение, nom.
190. Этой коробки, gen.
191. Машинистом, inst.; Железной дороге, prep.
192. Комнату, acc.;
193. Нашим родственникам, dat.
194. Социальным сетям, dat.
195. Москве, prep.; Новый парк, nom.
196. Бабушке, dat.; Врачу, dat.
197. Всем сотрудникам, dat.; Отчёт, acc.

198. Площади, prep.; Памятника, gen.
199. Чего, gen.; Им, dat.; Границу, acc.
200. Нам, dat.; Этой сложной задачи, gen.

Useful links

https://plusspeak.com/ - Online foreign language lessons, Online chat, textbooks. Author's website and blog. Learn and practice foreign languages.

https://www.amazon.com/dp/B01A74965S - Russian language in 25 lessons

https://www.amazon.com/dp/B01M4QHGOT - Russian Essential Grammar and Conversational language

http://morpher.ru/Demo.aspx - online case decliner

http://numeralonline.ru/ - online tool for declension of numerals

Made in the USA
Monee, IL
10 April 2024